THE
DEADLIEST LIES

ALSO BY ABRAHAM H. FOXMAN

Never Again? The Threat of the New Anti-Semitism

THE DEADLIEST LIES

THE ISRAEL LOBBY AND
THE MYTH OF JEWISH CONTROL

Abraham H. Foxman

THE DEADLIEST LIES

Copyright © Abraham H. Foxman, 2007.

All rights reserved. No part of this book may be used or reproduced in any manner whatsoever without written permission except in the case of brief quotations embodied in critical articles or reviews.

First published in 2007 by
PALGRAVE MACMILLAN™
175 Fifth Avenue, New York, N.Y. 10010 and
Houndmills, Basingstoke, Hampshire, England RG21 6XS.
Companies and representatives throughout the world.

PALGRAVE MACMILLAN is the global academic imprint of the Palgrave Macmillan division of St. Martin's Press, LLC and of Palgrave Macmillan Ltd. Macmillan® is a registered trademark in the United States, United Kingdom and other countries. Palgrave is a registered trademark in the European Union and other countries.

ISBN-13: 978–1–4039–8492–0
ISBN-10: 1–4039–8492–1

Library of Congress Cataloging-in-Publication Data

Foxman, Abraham H.
   The deadliest lies : the Israel lobby and the myth of Jewish control / Abraham H. Foxman.
      p.   cm.
   Includes bibliographical references.
   ISBN-13: 978–1–4039–8492–0
   ISBN-10: 1–4039–8492–1
   1. Jews—United States—Politics and government—21st century.
2. Jews—United States—Public opinion.   3. United States—Public opinion.   4. Antisemitism—United States—History—21st century.
5. United States—Foreign relations—Israel.   6. Israel—Foreign relations—United States.   7. Israel and the diaspora.   8. B'nai B'rith. Anti-defamation League.   I. Title.
E184.36.P64F69   2007
973'.04924—dc22

                                                                    2007016241

A catalogue record of the book is available from the British Library.

Design by Letra Libre, Inc.

First edition: September, 2007

10 9 8 7 6 5 4 3 2 1

Printed in the United States of America.

To my devoted wife Golda,
My cherished children, Michelle and Ariel,
And my son-in-law Dan,
For their love and support

To my dear grandchildren,
Leila, Gideon and Amirit,
Proud American Jews who love Israel

CONTENTS

ACKNOWLEDGMENTS

I HAD HOPED I WOULD NEVER HAVE TO WRITE A BOOK ON THIS subject. I wanted to believe that in our great democracy only those on the fringes of society would continue to engage in conspiracy theories about Jews. And while anti-Semitism certainly creeps beyond the fringe, it dramatically entered the mainstream when two prominent academics made the conspiratorial charges that American Jews, because of their own self-interest and concern for Israel, control American foreign policy and are responsible for the war in Iraq. These age-old canards had to be debunked, and thus *Deadliest Lies* had to be written.

Several people helped make this undertaking a reality and deserve acknowledgment.

I am especially indebted to Karl Weber for his understanding of me, my concerns, and the seriousness of the subject. He listened patiently and helped me translate my thoughts into this book. He is a true partner and a special friend.

I say thank you to my agent Lynne Rabinoff, who gave her support, enthusiasm, and dedication to the project. My publisher, Airié

Stuart of Palgrave Macmillian, was steadfast in her determination and commitment to getting this book published, and I thank her for it.

I am grateful to the Anti-Defamation League's current national chair, Glen S. Lewy, and past chair, Barbara B. Balser, for their support and faith in this project and in me.

A special thank you goes to several of my ADL colleagues who provided welcomed guidance and support throughout this undertaking: Ken Jacobson, for his wise counsel and insight; Michael Salberg, for his advice and acumen; Robert Sugarman for his thoughtful recommendations; and Myrna Shinbaum, who took charge of the project from beginning to end.

FOREWORD

by George P. Shultz

I N THIS IMPORTANT BOOK, ABE FOXMAN DOES WHAT HE HAS done his whole professional life: he defends groups and individuals—Jews and non-Jews—against defamatory lies. He has had plenty to do. People who hate seem unable to keep from lying about those whom they despise. Others cannot resist using lies and half-truths to exploit the hatred in others to advance their interests or agendas.

Abe Foxman is not arguing against criticism of Israel. If you want to hear harsh criticism of Israel's policies and leaders, listen to Israelis. It's a free, democratic, open, and relentlessly self-analytical place. So questioning Israel for its actions is legitimate, as part of a tough debate about national and international issues.

But lies are something else. Lies can be deadly. Throughout human history they have been used, not only to vilify, but to establish a basis for cruel and inhuman acts. Many groups and individuals have suffered as a result. The Jewish people have suffered most of all. The catalogue of lies about Jews is long and astonishingly crude, matched only by the suffering that has followed their promulgation.

The unique history of the Jewish people has, across the centuries, spawned the intellectual disease of anti-Semitism. Jews were persecuted as "perfidious" in the early Christian era, as insufferable zealots by the Romans, as sly exploiters by medieval Europeans, as financial manipulators during the rise of capitalism, as "rootless cosmopolitans" by Communists, and as "Communists" by Nazis. And all too often, the allegations sparked violence, brutality, and death on the Jews.

Thus defaming the Jews and disputing their rightful place among the peoples of the world has been a long-running, well-documented, and disgraceful series of episodes across history.

Again and again, a time has come when legitimate criticism slips across an invisible line into what might be called the "badlands," a place where those who should be regarded as worthy adversaries in debate are turned into scapegoats, targets, all-purpose objects of blame.

These moments become dangerous when otherwise respected and notable figures find themselves—knowingly or unthinkingly—slipping into such territory. The dangers expand exponentially if ignorant, prejudiced, or even deranged people act out their worst instincts and fantasies under the cover of authorization from such distinguished or prominent public figures.

In America, we protect all speech, even the most hurtful lies. Instead, we count on people such as Abe Foxman to challenge untruths and dangerous exaggerations with facts and reason. This is what he does in this book. It takes on three recent publications: a paper entitled "The Israel Lobby and U.S. Foreign Policy" by Professors John J. Mearsheimer of the University of Chicago and Stephen M. Walt of the John F. Kennedy School of Government at Harvard University; commentary on the same subject by New York University Professor Tony Judt; and former President Jimmy Carter's recent book, *Palestine: Peace Not Apartheid*. Many articles and books have examined these writings. This book clearly, vigorously, and succinctly details their flaws.

I have spent a good portion of my life serving in the government of the United States. I was a member of the Cabinet for a dozen years, six and one-half of them as Secretary of State. So I have had plenty of opportunity to see the workings of our system. We are a people committed to law. But we allow a virtual free-for-all in the process by which laws are adopted, enforced, and interpreted. Hundreds of millions of dollars are spent yearly to influence these processes. Thousands of groups vie for influence, pursuing the interests of many causes. Among these are the Jewish groups cited in the writings evaluated in this book as the all-powerful "Israel Lobby."

Jewish groups are influential. They also largely agree that the United States should support Israel. But the notion that these groups have anything like a uniform agenda, and that U.S. policy on Israel and the Middle East is the result of their influence, is simply wrong. The critics Abe Foxman takes on seem over-impressed with the way of thinking that says to itself, "Since there is this huge Arab-Islamic world out there with all the oil and it is opposed to this tiny little Israel with no natural resources, then realistically the United States has to be on the Arab side and against Israel on every issue, and since that isn't the case, there must be some underhanded Jewish plot at work." This is a conspiracy theory pure and simple, and scholars at great universities should be ashamed to promulgate it.

Then there is yet another tried and untrue method for damaging the well-being and security of the Jewish people and the State of Israel. This is the dangerously false analogy. The prominent recent case comes from former President Jimmy Carter's book *Palestine: Peace Not Apartheid.* Here the association, on the one hand, is between Israel's existentially threatened position and the measures it has taken to protect its population from terrorist attacks driven by an ideology bent on the complete eradication of the State of Israel, and, on the other, the racist oppression of South Africa's black population by the white Boer regime. Under sharp reactive criticism, President Carter has disavowed his choice of words, but the tendency of mind that lies behind such repulsive analogies remains and is reinforced by the former president's views, spread across his book, which come down on the anti-Israel side of every case. We must respect President Carter's clarification of his book but nonetheless bear in mind that once the false analogies start, it is only a short step to the cartoons in the Arab press and European media which portray Israelis as contemporary versions of Nazi storm troopers. And these false analogies stir up and lend legitimacy to more widely based movements that take the same dangerous direction, such as the deplorable recent proposals by British academic and other unions to boycott Israel.

Anyone who thinks that Jewish groups constitute a homogenous "lobby" ought to spend some time dealing with them. When Soviet persecution of Jews renewed in earnest after World War II, for example, Jewish groups were all over the place on what should be done. Some called for and funded the creation of a Jewish "homeland" within the Soviet Union. Some supported Israel's approach of quiet diplomacy. Most adopted the techniques of the civil rights movement and made lots of noise. Some advocated and used force. The tension among these groups—all dedicated to saving Soviet Jews—was electric. When the doors began to swing open, many American Jews wanted to allow the Soviet Jews to choose to come to the United States instead of going to Israel. Israel fought hard against these Jewish groups, arguing, among other things, that U.S. law should not discriminate against Israel as a haven for Jewish refugees. Many other examples could be cited, including my decision to open a dialogue with Yasser Arafat after he publicly met our longstanding conditions. My decision evoked a wide spectrum of responses from the government of Israel, its various political parties, and the many American Jewish groups who weighed in on one side or the other.

A number of examples can also be cited in which the U.S. rejected Israel's view of an issue, or the views of the American Jewish community. This book cites several, including the arms sales to Saudi Arabia. A very dramatic case was President Reagan's decision to go to the cemetery at Bitburg, Germany, on his trip to commemorate the end of the war in Europe and peace among former adversaries. When the decision was made, he did not know that the cemetery included SS officers of the Nazi machine. Jewish groups as well as the government of Israel protested vigorously. We looked hard at the issue. After hearing from Elie Wiesel and other great, moral figures, we concluded that the president should not go to Bitburg now that we knew who was buried there. But our important ally, Chancellor Helmut Kohl, had announced the trip. We asked if another site could be substituted for Bitburg. Chancellor Kohl said that he could not politically sustain that change. He had stood up courageously to his commitment for the deployment of Pershing missiles in Germany in late 1983, a turning point in the cold war. President Reagan concluded that America's interests required him to stand by his commitment. He did so, despite the pressure and understandable outrage directed against him. So, even where we agreed with the Jewish leadership, we were able to reject their position and act in America's best interests, as we judged them to be.

The United States supports Israel, not because of favoritism based on political pressure or influence, but because both political parties and virtually all our national leaders agree with the American people's view that supporting Israel is politically sound and morally just. Those who disagree with this policy, such as the authors whose writings are examined in this book, assume they cannot be wrong, and so they contend that the American people and its leadership must have been deceived, time and time again, by Israel and its supporters.

The United States has vigorously disagreed with many Israeli policies. We have made explicit our view, shared by most Israelis and American Jews, that a Palestinian state should be created alongside Israel. But any fair-minded person would have to recognize that Israel cannot achieve this objective without a Palestinian partner. When Egypt and Jordan were ready to make peace, Israel took the necessary steps and risks of doing so.

President Carter, more than anyone else, knows the great effort required for both Egypt and Israel to overcome years of warfare and hostility. He was instrumental in helping them to do so. His call for justice for Palestinians is heartfelt and sincere. But he knows better than to suggest that Israel has created a system of "apartheid" either within Israel or in the territories. Using this word is a dangerous exaggeration, and not an appropriate way to secure the attention he recently admitted he sought in doing so.

My problem with blaming Israel and the pro-Israel lobby for U.S. government policies and actions goes beyond the points ably made by Abe Foxman. We are a great nation, and our government officials invariably include brilliant, experienced, tough-minded people. Mostly, we make good decisions. But when we make a wrong decision—even one that is recommended by Israel and supported by American Jewish groups—it is our decision, and one for which we alone are responsible. We are not babes in the woods, easily convinced to support Israel's or any other state's agenda. We act in our own interests. And when we mistakenly conclude from time to time—as we will—that an action or policy is in America's interests, we must take responsibility for the mistake. We must take into account any effort to mislead us, as appeared to be the case with certain expatriates from Iraq. But we will fail far more frequently if we blame others for our mistakes than if we accept them as our own.

So, at every level, those who blame Israel and its Jewish supporters for U.S. policies they do not support are wrong. They are wrong because, to begin with, support for Israel is in our best interests. They are also wrong because Israel and its supporters have the right to try to influence U.S. policy. And they are wrong because the U.S. government is responsible for the policies it adopts, not any other state or any of the myriad lobbies and groups that battle daily—sometimes with lies—to win America's support.

It has taken not a little courage to write *The Deadliest Lies*. Perhaps what impresses me most of all is the fair-minded and carefully judicious tone of Abe Foxman's voice as it is heard in these pages. This is not an angry riposte, but the responsible and admirable effort by a good man to return the discourse to a civil, sane, and constructive level.

George P. Shultz
U. S. Secretary of State, 1982–1989
Thomas W. and Susan B. Ford Distinguished Fellow
Hoover Institution, Stanford University

I

IN A TIME OF CHALLENGE

T HIS IS A BOOK ABOUT FACTS, IDEAS, ATTITUDES, AND the links among them. It deals specifically with a recurring issue of vital importance not only to American Jews but to everyone who cares about this country and its relationships with the rest of the world—namely, the perceived tension between the love that most American Jews feel for their spiritual homeland, Israel, and their loyalty to the country whose citizenship they are proud to claim, the United States.

As you will see, this supposed tension is more apparent than real. The vast majority of American Jews experience no difficulty in being both loyal, patriotic Americans and supporters of Israel. They love both countries and want both to flourish. And virtually every time they face some choice concerning the policies or philosophy that either of their cherished countries should follow, they find it easy to identify a path that is beneficial to both nations—a path that leads toward ever-growing democracy, prosperity, and peace.

In a way, it is both strange and sad that I should have to explicitly state and defend this position. Very few Americans from other ethnic, religious, or national backgrounds are ever called upon to make a similar avowal. No one thinks to demand that Italian Americans or Greek Americans or German Americans or Americans who happen to be members of the Russian Orthodox church should have to declare their loyalty to this country, much less prove it. But for a complex set of reasons—some of them frankly related to religious prejudice and bigotry—American Jews find themselves in this position.

And today, in the early years of the twenty-first century, the demands that Jews *demonstrate* their love for and loyalty to the United States—and disavow any intention of betraying America's interests on behalf of a foreign land, specifically Israel—are a little louder and more insistent than usual.

Let's step back a bit to consider the historical context of this issue.

The relationship between the United States and the people of Israel actually predates the existence of the modern Israeli state. It has varied greatly during that time—sometimes closer, sometimes more distant; sometimes very friendly, sometimes wary, and sometimes even confrontational. As national goals, needs, and challenges change, so do perceptions of the national interest—and with them the policies pursued by the government on our behalf. In this sense, Israel has been like any other country with which the United States has a relationship.

But there are several unique elements in the case of Israel.

One of these is the special feeling that Americans have always had for Israel as "the Holy Land," the country of the Bible, the "Promised Land" of the Hebrew patriarchs whose words and deeds have been studied and revered by Christians everywhere.

I recently read the text of a remarkable address by Michael Oren, the American Israeli historian and author of the best-selling book *Six Days of War: June 1967 and the Making of the Modern Middle East.* In this address, Oren discusses the history of what he calls "restorationism," a philosophical movement that today is little known but had enormous popularity and influence in nineteenth-century America. It espoused the notion that there was a special kinship between the people of America and the Jews, and that one natural result of this kinship was a special obligation on the part of Americans to care for their Jewish brothers and sisters. More specifically, Americans had a calling from God to help the Jews escape from the long exile of the diaspora and return to the Holy Land—the "restoration" that gives "restorationism" its name. Oren explains:

> Perhaps the most . . . extraordinary expression of the restorationist idea appeared in a book published in 1844 called *The Valley of the Visions*[, which] called on the United States government to spearhead an international effort to detach Palestine from the Ottoman Empire and to give it back to the Jews as a State.

The Valley of the Visions became an antebellum bestseller; it sold about 1,000,000 copies and the author of that book was the Chairman of the Hebrew Department of New York University and his name was Professor George Bush, who was a direct . . . forebear . . . of two later American Presidents by the exact same name.[1]

Oren goes on to explain the influence of restorationism on notable Americans from Abraham Lincoln and Mark Twain to John D. Rockefeller and Emma Lazarus, the poet who wrote the famous verses that adorn the Statue of Liberty. Later, it played a role in the decision of President Woodrow Wilson to support the British promulgation of the Balfour Declaration, as well as in President Harry Truman's decision to make the United States the very first nation on earth to recognize the newly formed Jewish state.

Faith, then, has had a significant part in the American attitude toward Israel since long before the establishment of the nation in 1948. And there is little doubt it still affects the relationship between the two countries—most often in a positive way.

Another of these unique elements is the position of the American Jew. Because of Israel's special role as the homeland of the Jewish people, the relationship between Israel and the United States has been inextricably intertwined with the role and status of the Jews in American society. And this has created some special tensions and challenges for political leaders and ordinary citizens in calibrating the policies that govern U.S.-Israeli relations.

This aspect of the U.S.-Israel relationship isn't completely unparalleled. The United States is famously a melting pot, made up of immigrants from practically every nation on earth. Americans are proud of their varied ethnic and cultural backgrounds, and many bring their concerns about conditions in "the old country" to the table in their role as citizens of the United States with a voice in shaping the nation's foreign policy.

And this is true not only of first-generation immigrants or their children. Many Americans whose families have been in this country for generations retain strong ties of affection to and interest in their countries of origin. Just look at the Kennedys of Massachusetts, whose roots in the United States date back to the 1850s. To this day, Senator Edward Kennedy plays an especially active role in shaping U.S.-Irish relations and by speaking out on issues related to the Irish Republican Army, terrorism, and "the troubles" in Northern Ireland.

In most cases, we take this kind of concern in stride. It's sometimes a factor in domestic politics. For example, it's traditional for mayors of New York, one of the country's most ethnically diverse cities, to practically conduct a foreign policy of their own. Travels by mayors and even mayoral candidates to foreign lands to show their interest in and respect for the backgrounds of their domestic constituents are commonplace. At one time, these trips were especially focused on the so-called Three I's—Ireland, Italy, and Israel. Now, as the ethnic makeup of the city evolves, New York politicians are also displaying interest in such diverse lands as the Dominican Republic,

Vietnam, and the countries of western Africa—all sources of recent waves of immigration to the city. And none of this raises an eyebrow among observers of the city's politics.

But in some circles, the relationship between the Jews of America and the Jewish homeland of Israel has always been viewed a little differently than other ethnic ties. It has been considered a little less benign, a little more suspicious, a little more dangerous.

Why? One reason, of course, is because of the way Jews are often viewed. Outright anti-Semitism—hatred of Jews because of their religion or their perceived ethnic status—has declined in the United States in recent decades. But it is by no means a thing of the past, as recent statistics show. A 2005 survey of 1,600 American adults showed that about 14 percent hold views that can be described as "unquestionably anti-Semitic."[2] That translates to some 35 million people with anti-Semitic beliefs, a significant number by any standard.

Statistics, however, don't tell the whole story. Below the level of avowed anti-Semitism is a level of quiet, subtle bigotry—an attitude that may not rise to actual hatred of Jews but that assumes that Jews are somehow different, less respectable, less honorable, more treacherous, and more devious than other people. For those infected with this attitude, the fact of being a Jew is not a neutral or mildly interesting personal factor about someone, the way being red-headed or tall or left-handed—or a Methodist or a Baptist or a Lutheran—might be. Instead, this characteristic casts a social pall over its possessor, placing him or her in a different category, to be viewed and judged and treated differently from others.

This attitude toward the Jews—let's call it "bias" or "bigotry" rather than applying the stronger term "anti-Semitism"—is found, in some degree, in tens of millions of Americans. How many? It's hard to know for sure. But the polls find that perhaps as many as a third of adults have at least some degree of anti-Semitic belief, though not enough to qualify them as "strongly anti-Semitic."

And of course it's only natural that people who exhibit this kind of bias against Jews should look a little askance at the special relationship that exists between American Jews and the nation of Israel. After all, those who are predisposed to mistrust Jews take a negative view of many other forms of Jewish behavior—even to the point of being illogical and self-contradictory.

Is a particular Jew very sociable, with many friends of all religious and ethnic backgrounds? To the bigot, this demonstrates how "Jews are always pushing themselves forward and trying to ingratiate themselves where they don't belong." Is another Jew shy and stand-offish, perhaps appearing most comfortable only with family and a few close friends? To the bigot, this shows how "Jews are always sticking to their own kind because they think they're better than the rest of us."

Is a particular Jew successful in business—a banker, maybe, or a well-known lawyer or movie producer? To the bigot, this shows how "Jews are greedy, power-hungry capitalists, the kind who use free enterprise to exploit the world." Is another Jew an outspoken advocate of social justice and known for liberal political views? To the bigot, this shows how "Jews are left-wing agitators, closet communists trying to destroy the American free enterprise system."

If you're generally inclined to find fault with Jews no matter what they say or do—as the bigot is—then of course you will question the propriety of the American Jew's concern for the State of Israel. You won't think to compare it to the Italian American's love for the foods and cultural riches of Italy, the Irish American's longing for political freedom for his Irish relatives, the Brazilian American's pride in the triumphs of his country of origin on the soccer field, or the Chinese American's interest in the economic and social development of contemporary China.

All of those forms of pride and concern are considered harmless, even laudable. But the Jew's concern for Israel is something else. It is seen by some as a source of "dual loyalty." It is said to distort the American Jew's judgment about the politics of the Middle East and about international affairs generally. The leap is made that it leads American Jews to want to push their homeland, the United States, into policies and programs that are not in the best interests of America. In a worse scenario, this concern tempts Jews to commit treason—to seek to sacrifice the United States for the benefit of Israel.

This, then, is the assumption that the bigot will make when he thinks about American Jews and their attitude toward Israel. And as the bigot always does, he will look for every scrap of evidence that seems to support his assumption and ignore a mountain of evidence that might undermine it. He tends to read newspapers, magazines, and Internet sites that agree with his point of view, and to listen to TV and radio broadcasts that take the same position. So the longer he lives and the more he "learns" about Israel, the Middle East, and U.S. foreign policy, the more firmly he becomes convinced that American Jews are some-how untrustworthy on this issue—that they alone, of all the American ethnic and religious groups, have no legitimate right to an opinion about government policy in a particular area of interest to them.

I hasten to point out that many, many Americans are *not* bigoted in this way. Many Americans are entirely fair-minded in their atti-tudes toward Jews. They know that Jews, like Episcopalians and Hin-dus and Muslims and atheists, are human beings with the flaws and virtues and mixed characters that all human beings exhibit. And they understand that American Jews have a special interest in the survival and success of Israel, just as Americans of Norwegian or Turkish or Spanish descent have a special interest in the well-being of Norway or Turkey or Spain.

But the fact that millions of Americans *do* accept the bigot's point of view—in some cases without thinking about it very much or being particularly conscious of it—inevitably creates a certain tension sur-rounding discussions of U.S. policy toward Israel and the Middle East. People, especially politicians and pundits in the media, think of Israel as one of those hot buttons around which controversy tends to swirl and that people need to be "careful" about discussing publicly lest they offend someone or other.

The fact that the Jewish community in America is relatively suc-cessful, articulate, and politically involved helps to deepen this sense that Israel is a hot button.

Even in this regard, Israel isn't completely unique. In recent years, American policy toward Cuba has become a comparably hot button.

The parallels to the Israel debate are interesting. Cuban Americans are a relatively successful and outspoken group. They are geographically concentrated in a few places, especially southern Florida, which gives them some political clout. (If they were to vote in high proportions for or against a particular candidate, they might sway a close election.) And just as most Jews have at least some degree of concern about Israel—and some are passionately concerned—so, too, most Cuban Americans have at least some concern over the fate of their island homeland and the quest of many of its people for freedom from communist rule, while some are passionately devoted to the anti-Castro cause. For these reasons, the "Cuban American lobby" is sometimes seen as inordinately powerful, and controversy has sometimes erupted over the degree to which this lobby affects U.S. policy.

This is, perhaps, the closest parallel to the situation in which Jewish American lovers of Israel find themselves. But even this comparison isn't exact. Because the Jews themselves are "controversial" in the minds and hearts of some Americans, Jewish advocacy on behalf of causes they believe in—including Israel—will always be controversial too. To put it more bluntly, there have always been Americans—and perhaps always will be some—who wish that their Jewish fellow citizens would just sit down and shut up.

This sense of antagonism toward Jewish advocacy is naturally heightened during times of intense global conflict—particularly when that conflict involves Israel and the Middle East, either directly or indirectly.

There's a history of blaming the Jews for American involvement in foreign wars that dates back to at least World War II. It's as if the isolationists, who imagine that the United States should somehow be untouched by global conflicts that affect every other major power on earth, believe that it is the Jews and the Jews alone who cause us to be entangled in world affairs.

In the years immediately preceding the American entry into World War II, right-wing Republicans like Charles Lindbergh and the America First Committee opposed American involvement in the conflict. They claimed that the struggle against fascism was a purely European squabble, none of our business, and that only Jews wanted the United States to intervene in the hopes that we could save them from Nazi tyranny. For example, in a now-notorious speech in Des Moines, Iowa, on September 11, 1941—less than three months before Pearl Harbor—Charles Lindbergh said:

> Instead of agitating for war, the Jewish groups in this country should be opposing it in every possible way for they will be among the first to feel its consequences.
>
> Tolerance is a virtue that depends upon peace and strength. History shows that it cannot survive war and devastations. A few far-sighted Jewish people realize this and stand opposed to intervention. But the majority still do not.
>
> Their greatest danger to this country lies in their large ownership and influence in our motion pictures, our press, our radio and our government.[3]

The fact that the Lindbergh crowd was comfortable with anti-Semitic bigotry and had more than flirted with supporting Hitler and the other fascist powers made this position come naturally to them.

For a time, the America First Committee was remarkably success-ful at attracting attention and prominent supporters. Its president was General Robert Wood, the legendary business genius who served as CEO of Sears, Roebuck, then the nation's premier retailing company. Others who served on its executive board included Alice Longworth Roosevelt (Teddy's daughter), Robert Maynard Hutchins (president of the University of Chicago), actress Lillian Gish, and America's greatest industrialist, Henry Ford—who was also an avowed anti-Semite.

You might wonder how American Jews responded to this rather intimidating coalition of isolationists, Nazi-appeasers, and semibigots. The answer is: not very effectively. By the 1930s, the large numbers of Eastern European Jews who had migrated to North America around the turn of the century had carved out places for themselves in the cul-ture of the United States. But Jews *as Jews* were a largely invisible pres-ence on the American scene. Here is how historian Walter Laqueur describes their status:

> As for Jewish political influence, it was nearly nonexistent or, at best, insufficient to help open the gates of America a little wider for refugees from Nazism in the 1930s. By that time, Jews had attained leading positions in the print media, pub-lishing, and the entertainment industry, especially in Holly-wood, but out of fear of antisemitism they leaned over backward not to promote any specific Jewish concerns. To give but two examples: the *New York Times*, which was in Jew-ish hands, had very little to report about the mass murder of European Jewry during World War Two, and Hollywood moguls were equally silent.[4]

The case of the *New York Times* is an especially interesting one for several reasons. The *Times* is the most prestigious and widely respected newspaper in the United States and is often described as "the paper of record." It has long been owned by Jewish Americans (Adolph Ochs, publisher of the *Chattanooga Times,* purchased the paper in 1896, and it has remained in his family ever since), and therefore has long been subject to special scrutiny for supposed ethnic or religious influence. For at least the last three decades, it has been subject to attacks, especially from the far right, for its supposed "liberal bias."

In fact, one might assume, based on the volume of criticism the *New York Times* receives, that its pages have long been filled with slanted information and scarcely veiled propaganda on behalf of "Jewish causes" and left-wing politics. (As we'll see later, such criticism has hardly abated. It plays a part in the current spate of supposedly scholarly studies of "overweening Jewish influence" that is a central focus of this book.)

The facts are quite otherwise. As the most mainstream of mainstream media outlets, the *New York Times* has always prided itself on "playing the news straight down the middle," even when this seemed to require a deliberate downplaying of stories that the editors' journalistic instincts rightly deemed important. This applied, as Laqueur suggests, to the Holocaust itself, by any measure one of the two or three most significant historical events of the twentieth century.

How did this happen? Here is the explanation offered by Laurel Leff, a professor of journalism at Northeastern University and author of *Buried by The Times: The Holocaust and America's Most Important Newspaper:*

> ... the American media in general and the *New York Times* in particular never treated the Holocaust as an important news story. From the start of the war in Europe to its end nearly six years later, the story of the Holocaust made the *Times* front page only 26 times out of 24,000 front-page stories, and most of those stories referred to the victims as "refugees" or "persecuted minorities." In only six of those stories were Jews identified on page one as the primary victims.
>
> Nor did the story lead the paper, appearing in the right-hand column reserved for the day's most important news—not even when the concentration camps were liberated at the end of the war. In addition, the *Times* intermittently and timidly editorialized about the extermination of the Jews, and the paper rarely highlighted it in either the "Week in Review" or the magazine section. ... [Because of its strong connections to the Jewish community,] the *New York Times* was less likely than other news organizations to miss what was happening to the Jews. But it was also more likely to dismiss its significance. Fearful of accusations of special pleading or dual loyalties, the newspaper hesitated to highlight the news. In addition, the newspaper's Jewish publisher believed that Jews were neither a racial nor ethnic group, and therefore should not be identified as Jews for any other than religious reasons. He also believed that Americans would only want to help Jews if their cause was melded with that of other persecuted people. He therefore ensured that his paper universalized the Nazis' victims in editorials and on the front page.

The result: *The New York Times* was in touch with European Jews' suffering, which accounts for its 1,000-plus stories on the Final Solution's steady progress. Yet, it deliberately de-emphasized the Holocaust news, reporting it in isolated, inside stories. The few hundred words about the Nazi genocide the *Times* published every couple [of] days were hard to find amidst a million other words in the newspaper. *Times* readers could legitimately have claimed not to have known, or at least not to have understood, what was happening to the Jews.[5]

It's ironic that anti-Semites like Henry Ford, and those like Lindbergh who flirted with anti-Semitism, were obsessed with fears of "Jewish influence" subverting American culture. Yet the handful of Jews with an actual opportunity, through the press, to affect how Americans thought and felt were extremely reluctant to use that opportunity, largely because they were intimidated by the veiled and not-so-veiled threats they sensed from the Jew-baiters on the right. To exaggerate only a little, merely *talking* about the "menace of Jewish mind control" was enough to virtually extinguish any real Jewish influence on the attitudes of the day.

Thankfully, despite the hesitation of much of the mass media to define the threat of anti-Semitism accurately and frankly, the vast majority of Americans rejected the America First-ers. They saw the Nazi threat for what it was, a danger to every democratic nation on earth, and they supported the war not because they were worried about the fate of the Jews but because they didn't want to live in a world ruled by Hitler and his minions. Still, the isolationists' propaganda had an impact. And the seed they planted of pernicious assumptions about Jewish "dual loyalty" and the readiness of the Jews to sacrifice American lives for their own alien purposes grew in the darkness, until another international crisis would give it an opportunity to find the light of day.

In 1991, when the United States led a coalition of nations in the Gulf War in order to free Kuwait from control by Iraq, a new breed of quasi isolationists came out in force to blame the Jews. Most of them were too careful to use overtly anti-Semitic language. Instead, they employed coded terminology. Republican luminary, television pundit, and one-time presidential candidate Pat Buchanan exemplified the technique. Buchanan, a true heir of the old-time isolationists and an admirer of Lindbergh, once remarked in an interview:

> There was nothing immoral, or unwise, about the isolationists' position of 1940–41. Because of the courageous efforts of Lindbergh and America First, the United States stayed out of the war until Hitler threw the full force of his war machine against Stalin. Thus, the Soviet Union, not America's young, bore the brunt of defeating Nazi Germany.[6]

Now, following in the footsteps of his hero, Buchanan used his pulpit as a leading political commentator to denounce the Gulf War as an unnecessary conflict that only the Jews would benefit from. On a June 15, 1990, broadcast of the syndicated television talk show *The McLaughlin Group,* on which Buchanan had a regular berth, he proclaimed, "Capitol Hill is Israeli occupied territory." On the September 15, 1990, show, he declared, "there are only two groups that are beating the drums for war in the Middle East—the Israeli defense ministry and its 'amen corner' in the United States." Then he added, "The Israelis want this war desperately because they want the United States to destroy the Iraqi war machine. They want us to finish them off. They don't care about our relations with the Arab world."[7]

Again, the isolationist, anti-Jewish voices did not prevail. The United States did indeed intervene in the Persian Gulf, successfully driving the Iraqi armies out of Kuwait and (as we now know) effectively containing Saddam Hussein's ambitions for greater regional hegemony. But again the seed of anti-Jewish sentiment was nurtured and strengthened. The idea that American Jews were somehow agents of Israel, ready to advocate policies detrimental to the United States in order to help a foreign country, was given fresh prominence and a new lease on life.

With this historical and cultural context, we can see how the horrific events of September 11, 2001—a painful turning point in the history of the world and of the United States in particular—created unique problems for American Jews. The reason: A world in which fears of terrorism generated by 9/11 are a shaping force in U.S. foreign policy is a world in which the role of Israel—and by extension the role of American Jews in the national debate—is bound to stir up powerful emotions: fear, resentment, anger. And this is exactly what we see happening today, with consequences for the public debate that are very disturbing—and even dangerous.

2

OLD POISON IN A NEW BOTTLE

O N SEPTEMBER 11, 2001, THE WESTERN WORLD ENTERED A new era of anxiety, uncertainty, and fear.

For a decade or more, thoughtful people in Europe, North America, and the rest of the developed world had been wrestling with a series of dramatic changes that had seemed to portend a time of almost unlimited hope. In the autumn of 1989, the Berlin Wall—that unparalleled symbol of the cold war—had come crashing down, and in the wake of its fall, a tide of freedom had surged across the formerly captive states of Eastern Europe. *Glasnost, perestroika,* and the collapse of the Soviet economy had spelled an end to the communist dominance of the East, and Russia was in the process of morphing from a global threat into a midsized economic and political power trying to cope with enormous internal problems, from horrific environmental degradation to a dwindling birth rate. As totalitarian regimes gave way to fledgling democracies, their peoples plunged enthusiastically if inexpertly into the modern world of consumer markets and popular self-government, and the postwar landscape of two Europes separated by barbed wire and tank battalions seemed ripe for transformation into a vibrant, unified continent of prosperous democracies.

These political upheavals were accompanied by an almost equally momentous series of economic and technological changes. With the death of the false idol of communism, the ideology and practice of free markets swept the planet. Vast countries once seemingly trapped forever in poverty, from China and India to Indonesia and Brazil, turned wholeheartedly to modern capitalism, and new markets made up of tens of millions of newly middle-class citizens began to emerge. Revolutions in communication and information technology, from the cell phone and the personal computer to satellite television and the Internet, brought Western-style news and entertainment into homes on every continent. Instantaneous electronic connections made it possible for shoestring businesses to sell their products and services to giant corporations halfway around the globe—and, in time, to compete with those corporations in their own right. It was a heady, exciting time.

Then, on 9/11, the terrorists struck. And the bright world of new possibilities ushered in by the last decade of the twentieth century suddenly revealed its dark side.

The looming threat of nuclear attack by the nations of the former Soviet bloc had diminished. But now a new threat took its place: the threat of terrorism originating in the developing world but seemingly able to strike anywhere at any time with lethal force.

In itself, terrorism was nothing new. Fringe political movements had used stealthy violent attacks as a tactic for instilling fear in their enemies and drawing attention to their causes since the nineteenth century. Even the specific threat of terror attacks by Islamist extremists on Western targets was not unfamiliar.* But the scale and audacity of the 9/11 attacks raised the stakes enormously. As Americans and their friends around the world watched the twin towers of the World Trade Center collapse, they recognized the true depth of their vulnerability. Terrible as the destruction of 9/11 was, it took little imagination to conjure up far worse nightmares: terrorists with chemical or biological weapons, or with one or two of the "loose nukes" that the end of the cold war had suddenly rendered accessible.

A world of hope and limitless opportunities was transformed overnight into a world of paranoia and fear.

---

* Like many others, I use the term *Islamist* with a specific meaning. It describes extreme adherents of Islam who accept a fundamentalist interpretation of the Koran; favor the imposition of strict Islamic law *(sharia)* in Muslim countries; regard the Judeo-Christian West as culturally, socially, and politically corrupt; and believe in the use of violence, even against civilians, in pursuit of their objectives. The term should *not* be interpreted as a condemnation of the Muslim faith, to which I refer using the neutral descriptive term *Islamic.*

For many people in the West, the *nature* of this new, unexpected threat made it especially frightening. Despite its great power, the Soviet Union had been a familiar kind of adversary: a nation-state whose leaders could be negotiated with, appealed to on the basis of economic and political self-interest, and, when necessary, threatened with overwhelming force. The doctrine of mutually assured destruction struck many as disturbing and perhaps unstable—like a global game of chicken with the survival of humankind at stake—but it had kept the peace, more or less, for fifty years.

The Islamist terror threat seemed very different. Its leaders were not statesmen or politicians; they had no citizenry to answer to, no economy to safeguard, no territory to defend. The suicidal nature of their attacks—not just on 9/11 but also in the bombings that had already afflicted cities in Europe and the Middle East, especially Israel—made it clear that the threat of reprisals would be a far less effective deterrent to terrorists than it had been to the Soviet Union. Most alarming of all, the motivations of the Islamists were difficult for many in the West even to comprehend—a mix of social, political, ethnic, and religious resentments and visions that seemed like something out of the Middle Ages come back to haunt us in the twenty-first century, now armed with the most powerful modern technologies.

If the images of 9/11 on our television screens had struck millions of viewers as being like scenes from a science-fiction thriller, the permanent state of anxiety that our new awareness of the terror threat induced felt like a nightmare out of a cheap horror movie—except that this was a nightmare from which we couldn't wake up.

As the last remaining superpower and as the nation struck by the 9/11 attacks, the United States naturally took the lead in formulating the West's response to this new threat. A young and relatively inexperienced president, George W. Bush, was at the helm. And at first, the citizens of this country and those of America's traditional allies rallied around him in unity and support. In October 2001, forces of the United States and other NATO members invaded Afghanistan, which had served as a training center and operational base for al-Qaeda, the terrorist group believed to be responsible for the 9/11 attacks. Most of the world, including the leadership of the United Nations, expressed their approval. By the end of the year, most of Afghanistan had fallen to the forces of the Western coalition. The extreme Islamist group known as the Taliban, an ally of al-Qaeda, had been driven from power. Al-Qaeda's chief financial backer and mastermind, Osama bin Laden, had managed to escape, but it was assumed that his capture was only a matter of time.

Unfortunately, the sense that the West was united behind a leader with a clear and powerful vision for dealing with the Islamist threat would be short-lived.

In March 2003, the Bush administration led a handful of its staunchest allies into a war that was far more controversial than the war in Afghanistan. This was the war to topple Saddam Hussein, the widely feared and hated dictator of Iraq. And while the initial phase of the invasion was highly successful—Saddam was driven from power within a matter of weeks—in retrospect, the launch of the Iraq war marked the beginning of an even more difficult and troubling time for the United States and the West.

This book isn't the place for me to enter the ongoing debate about the Iraq war. It's a controversy that will undoubtedly continue for decades. In the months leading up to the invasion, the Bush administration offered a series of strategic and political rationales for the war. Chief among them was the international threat posed by the arsenal of chemical and biological weapons that Saddam Hussein's regime was generally assumed to maintain, as well as by the nuclear weapons program many experts believed he was developing. In the aftermath of the invasion, with the discovery that Iraq apparently had no such arsenal, many in the United States and around the world have complained that they were duped into war. And as the relatively easy victories of 2003 have given way to an increasingly costly, dangerous, and less-hopeful situation in Iraq—with an unstable government, a persistent and deadly insurgency, and ethnic and religious rivalries exerting a seemingly unstoppable centrifugal force—millions of Americans have come to believe that the war itself was a huge mistake. For them, the enormous drain on the U.S. treasury (estimated at some $2 billion plus per week) and the painful cost in American lives (3,500 and counting) has been a terrible waste.

Other Americans, by contrast, continue to defend President Bush and the decision to go to war—even as they criticize many aspects of the administration's conduct of the war.

The nation and the world are bitterly divided over Iraq. No one is happy with the current situation, but no clear consensus as to what the United States and its allies should do in the near future has emerged. And as Americans and their friends around the world argue over Iraq, the uncertainty, anger, and resentment spill over into other issues related to the Middle East and U.S. foreign policy in general. How should we deal with the growing danger from another rogue state in the region, an Islamist Iran that is actively seeking nuclear weapons? What role should the United States play in seeking a settlement of the festering Palestinian-Israeli conflict? Should the United States engage in diplomacy with regimes like the one in Syria, which has played a dangerously destabilizing role in the region? Should we maintain our alliances with such powerful but nondemocratic Arab states as Saudi Arabia, which provoke enormous resentment from the Islamists? And how will our decisions on all these complex issues affect our vulnerability, and that of our allies, to future terrorist attacks?

The world of the cold war was a dangerous and scary place. But by the mid-2000s, many in the West were looking back on those days almost with nostalgia. In retrospect, the choices we faced then seemed simpler, the path clearer, the dangers more manageable, the distinctions between "good guys" and "bad guys" easier to comprehend.

In this new and troubling world, it was perhaps inevitable that recriminations, scare mongering, and finger pointing should take place. They happened during the cold war, too, of course; you may recall the debates over "Who lost China?" and the accusations over the existence or nonexistence of communist infiltrators in the U.S. government. But in today's hyperpartisan Washington, in a world already on edge, and with the new electronic media creating ever-faster news cycles and instant debates on every topic, it's not surprising that the arguments over "Who got us into this mess?" should have arisen even more quickly and more vociferously than during the 1950s.

And as history shows us, when people in the West are sufficiently anxious, fearful, angry, and confused, a familiar scapegoat tends to rise to the surface again and again: the Jews.

In the past, periods of Jew baiting have been launched from many quarters—by governments eager to deflect blame from their own failures, by clerics using age-old hatreds to draw attention and attract congregations, by writers and speechmakers and radio personalities, such as Father Coughlin, appealing to bigotry.

In 2006, two mild-mannered university professors inaugurated a new era of anti-Jewish scapegoating—whether they did it intentionally or not.

In March of 2006, John J. Mearsheimer, of the University of Chicago, and Stephen M. Walt, of the John F. Kennedy School of Government at Harvard, published an article entitled "The Israel Lobby and U.S. Foreign Policy." It appeared originally as a working paper on the website of the Kennedy School; later, it was published in a somewhat shorter, revised version in the *London Review of Books*, a highly regarded magazine of social, artistic, literary, and political criticism that is read throughout the world.

Every year, hundreds of articles on U.S. foreign policy are published in a wide array of specialized publications, and most sink without a trace. The Mearsheimer-Walt article, however, provoked a different reaction. It created a controversy that has reverberated for months and shows no sign of abating even today, more than a year after its initial publication. It has generated heated debate among thousands of academics, students, pundits, policymakers, and interested citizens, and undoubtedly has shifted the thinking of many people around the world—for good or ill.

The inescapable message presented by Mearsheimer and Walt was an explosive, inflammatory one. The fact that such a startling message would be delivered in a respected journal of opinion would, all by itself, attract attention and controversy. But the article would not have been taken seriously if not for the reputations and associations of the authors, each of whom has written respected scholarly works on government and international relations and occupies an important position at his university. Mearsheimer, a West Point graduate and a professor at the University of Chicago, is the author of three books, including *The Tragedy of Great Power Politics,* while Walt, who was the academic dean of the Kennedy School, is the author of *Taming American Power: The Global Response to U.S. Primacy.*

It is because of their reputations and the fame of the institutions with which they are associated that their article has created such a stir. Many who have read it—especially those with expertise in the history of the Middle East and the details of American foreign policy, among them Eliot Cohen and former ambassadors Dennis Ross and Martin Indyk—have recognized the article's numerous distortions, omissions, and errors. Many took the time to write critiques and replies that, taken together, go a long way toward demolishing the credibility of the article. Questions about the motives of Mearsheimer and Walt have also been raised.

Unfortunately, many who read the article or hear about its main arguments secondhand lack the background knowledge to evaluate it accurately. Some of these people will be misled by Mearsheimer and Walt. Taking the authors' impressive credentials as a guarantee of quality, they may assume that the ideas in the article are valid and the "evidence" presented is truthful. And a few who are predisposed to support any message that is unfavorable to Israel or to the Jewish people will latch onto the article with glee as validation for their own bigoted views. (Indeed, we have already seen this happening, as I'll detail later in this chapter.)

For this reason, the Mearsheimer-Walt controversy deserves the attention I'm giving it here. Indeed, it was the furor created by the article that first prompted me to consider writing this book. And there's every reason to believe that the controversy is not going away. Mearsheimer and Walt have parlayed the notoriety created by their article into a contract with a prestigious American book publisher. Their book-length explication of their thesis is currently scheduled for publication toward the end of 2007. Undoubtedly it will generate an even greater round of attention and controversy than the original article. And, unfortunately, the book will probably win further converts to the authors' position. For this reason, too, a strong response from those who disagree is imperative.

The basic thesis of Mearsheimer and Walt is stated on the very first page:

> For the past several decades . . . and especially since the Six-Day War in 1967, the centerpiece of U.S. Middle East policy has been its relationship with Israel. The combination of unwavering U.S. support for Israel and the related effort to spread democracy throughout the region has inflamed Arab and Islamic opinion and jeopardized U.S. security.
>
> This situation has no equal in American political history. Why has the U.S. been willing to set aside its own security in order to advance the interests of another state? One might assume that the bond between the two countries is based on shared strategic interests or compelling moral imperatives. As we show below, however, neither of these explanations can account for the remarkable level of material and diplomatic support that the U.S. provides to Israel.
>
> Instead, the overall thrust of U.S. policy in the region is due almost entirely to U.S. domestic politics, and especially to the activities of the "Israel Lobby." Other special interest groups have managed to skew U.S. foreign policy in directions they favored, but no lobby has managed to divert U.S. foreign policy as far from what the American national interest would otherwise suggest, while simultaneously convincing Americans that U.S. interests and Israeli interests are essentially identical.[1]

The article attempts to demonstrate this thesis through a series of assertions, citing a grab bag of historical examples, quotations from various political and government figures, and supposedly revealing facts and incidents. The overall thread of Mearsheimer and Walt's argument is:

- That the State of Israel has no moral standing on which to claim support from the United States;
- That the strategic importance of Israel as an American supporter is also insufficient to explain the closeness of the alliance between the two countries;
- That, therefore, some less-straightforward explanation must be sought;
- That the only logical explanation is the unprecedented power of the Israel Lobby, which has succeeded in bending U.S. policymakers both in Congress and in successive administrations to its will despite the fact that the policies it advocates run directly contrary to the best interests of the United States;
- And that, furthermore, this Israel Lobby is so powerful that it has been able to virtually eliminate honest debate about Israeli policies and the U.S.-Israel alliance, censoring and stifling free speech on these issues and preventing Americans from hearing all sides of the debate on the future of the Middle East.

As you can see, Mearsheimer and Walt are tackling some very big topics. One would think that so broad and sweeping an indictment of the political system of the world's leading democracy would demand a deeply scholarly, thoughtful approach based on careful analysis of the most reliable historical sources and a balanced survey of expert voices on all sides of the issues. So one would think. Unfortunately, the article that Mearsheimer and Walt actually wrote doesn't take such an approach. Instead, it addresses many of the most important and complicated issues surrounding the Middle East conflict in a perfunctory and all-knowing fashion. Nowhere in evidence is a sense of complexity and balance, a nuanced examination of the variety of factors that generally underlie most historical events, or any attempt to put individual comments in perspective—all the appropriate tools for a serious piece of scholarship or journalism.

Instead, on issue after issue, the authors start with unproven, anti-Israel assumptions and then point to isolated examples to justify these assumptions. One does not have to take a pro-Israel position to recognize that the authors, despite their reputations, have no interest in producing a serious, balanced work. The result is a sloppy diatribe—a fact that many observers who *endorse* all or part of the Mearsheimer-Walt analysis have been forced to admit.

For example, Michael Massing, a contributing editor of the *Columbia Journalism Review,* wrote a follow-up article titled "The Storm over the Israel Lobby." Massing is largely supportive of Mearsheimer and Walt. In his article, he praises them for "forcing into the open a subject that has for too long remained taboo." Yet in the same article, Massing also has to acknowledge that "The Israel Lobby" contains "factual errors," uses quotations "badly out of context," follows "an unconvincing line of reasoning," and exhibits a "tendency to emphasize

Israel's offenses while largely overlooking those of its adversaries." Massing concludes, "it would take a much fuller and [more] richly sourced discussion than the one presented by the authors to make their case seem convincing."[2]

If this is what your *friends* say about you, what is left for your opponents to say?

My years at the Anti-Defamation League have made me realistic. I'm well aware that the world contains some die-hard anti-Semites who will never read anything I write—or, if they do, will simply scour the pages in hope of finding some tiny inconsistency or error that they can use to discredit my entire message. I'm not writing for their benefit. They have already taken Mearsheimer and Walt to their bosom, and nothing I say will convince them to change their attitude.

So the anti-Semites already know where they stand in relation to Mearsheimer and Walt: They are delighted with the pair's thesis and see in it support for much of what they believe. This chapter, and indeed this entire book, is addressed to a different audience: fair-minded people who may be wondering whether there is any truth in the claims promoted in "The Israel Lobby" and are willing to hear the other side of the story.

I know that bigoted individuals and groups will happily disseminate the Mearsheimer-Walt article, and they will circulate selected quotations and "facts" from its pages for decades to come. They'll use print media, broadcasting, and the Internet to spread its ideas as widely as possible. My message will probably reach fewer people. Plain facts and complex realities aren't as sexy as conspiracy theories and black-and-white accusations. But it's important to put the truth out there—and to have faith that, in the long run, it will prevail.

Please note that I am *not* calling Mearsheimer and Walt "anti-Semites." I don't want the discussion of their article and their thinking to get sidetracked into parsing the precise meaning of that abhorrent term. But I am saying that their article repeats and supports myths and beliefs that anti-Semites have peddled for centuries, thereby giving aid and comfort to some of the most despicable people in our society. And it does so not by revealing an "inconvenient truth"—to borrow a phrase from another controversial context—but by using half-truths, distortions, and falsehoods to prop up a general analysis that is dishonest and wrong.

Here, in a nutshell, is how "The Israel Lobby" works: Mearsheimer and Walt start by blaming Israel for everything in the Israeli-Palestinian conflict. Having established Israel's consistent guilt from the creation of the state to the present day, they then move to asserting that the American "Israel Lobby" (which is loosely and inconsistently defined) uses every device and method of pressure politics to stifle criticism of Israel and to ensure that the United States adheres to a blindly pro-Israel policy, against America's true interests and to serve the interests of the Jewish State.

Let's examine some of the distortions and half-truths that Mearsheimer and Walt employ in support of their dubious thesis.

On Israel's founding, they cite as truth several of the most extreme anti-Israel perspectives. They write, for example, of Israel's "crimes" against the Palestinians in the creation of the state, describing, in particular, how "Jewish forces drove up to 700,000 Palestinians into exile."[3] This is, at best, a very cursory, one-sided description of a complex sequence of historic events, one that fair-minded scholars have studied and debated for years, freely criticizing Israel when such criticism is warranted. Were some Palestinians forced from the land by Jewish soldiers? Yes. Did others leave voluntarily, at the urging of Arab leaders? Did still others flee simply to escape the random violence that, tragically, always accompanies war? Yes, and yes again. But Mearsheimer and Walt don't seem to be interested in a balanced account. They cherry-pick facts that serve their purpose while disregarding or distorting the rest. The Jews were wrong, and that's the end of the discussion.

The authors' use of quotations from the historical record is similarly slanted. For example, they select an out-of-context quotation from David Ben-Gurion, the first prime minister of Israel, to "prove" that Israel did not actually accept the partition of Palestine into Jewish and Arab states: "After the formation of a large army in the wake of the establishment of the state, we shall abolish partition and expand to the whole of Palestine." Yes, Ben-Gurion said these words. But when he was asked, in a follow-up question, whether he meant to achieve this by force, he replied, "Through mutual understanding and Jewish-Arab agreement."[4] You won't find this clarification cited by Mearsheimer and Walt.

Here is another example. In an effort to demonstrate Israel's historic indifference to the rights and concerns of the Palestinians, Mearsheimer and Walt declare, "Prime Minister Golda Meir famously remarked that 'there was no such thing as a Palestinian.'"[5] Again, the bare words are quoted accurately, but the context is omitted and the meaning obfuscated. In the 1969 *Sunday Times* (London) interview that Mearsheimer and Walt are quoting, Meir was asked whether she considered "the emergence of the Palestinian fighting forces, the Fedayeen, an important new factor in the Middle East." Her reply:

> Important, no. A new factor, yes. There was no such thing as Palestinians. When was there an independent Palestinian people with a Palestinian state? It was either southern Syria before the First World War, and then it was a Palestine including Jordan. It was not as though there was a Palestinian people in Palestine considering itself as a Palestinian people and we came and threw them out and took their country away from them. They did not exist.[6]

The complete response makes it clear that Meir was talking not about the existence of Palestinians as individuals or even as a group, but of the existence of a Palestinian *nation*. And she was stating a simple fact—that prior to the late 1960s, no one, least of all the other Arab nations, had recognized the existence or even the potential existence of such a nation. Hence, as she said, the emergence of a Palestinian fighting force represented "a new factor" in the Middle East.

Could Meir have made her point more clearly? Probably. And she paid dearly for her lack of clarity. Over the years, her words have been repeatedly cited by anti-Zionists (and sometimes by outright anti-Semites) to "demonstrate" the dismissiveness of Israeli leaders toward the Palestinian people. No matter how often Meir later sought to clarify her meaning, the quotation was too useful for the biased to abandon. It's disturbing to see authors with a reputation for scholarship misusing it in the same old way.

No wonder historian Benny Morris, whom Mearsheimer and Walt repeatedly cite as a source for their historical information, felt driven to respond. Morris is not an unthinking apologist for Israel. In books such as *The Birth of the Palestinian Refugee Problem, 1947–1949,* he has harshly criticized Israeli actions and even claimed evidence for Israeli atrocities during the founding of the nation. Yet, disturbed by Mearsheimer's and Walt's misuse of his writings, Morris has written:

> Like many pro-Arab propagandists at work today, Mearsheimer and Walt often cite my own books, sometimes quoting directly from them, in apparent corroboration of their arguments. Yet their work is a travesty of the history that I have studied and written for the past two decades. Their work is riddled with shoddiness and defiled by mendacity. Were "The Israel Lobby and U.S. Foreign Policy" an actual person, I would have to say that he did not have a single honest bone in his body.[7]

Mearsheimer and Walt are equally biased when they write about the issues of peace, including recent and current efforts at finding a solution to the protracted, violent, and tragic standoff between the Palestinians and the Israelis. Assuming that Israel has never been serious about reconciliation with the Palestinians, the authors work hard to find ways to dismiss Israeli offers to the Palestinians.

Most notable is their denigration of the offer made by Prime Minister Ehud Barak and U.S. president Bill Clinton to Yasser Arafat at Camp David in 2000, saying that it provided the Palestinians not with the land on which to establish a state but merely a collection of "Bantustans."[8] The word is, of course, a reference to the phony "homelands" created by the abhorrent apartheid government in South Africa as a way of isolating and controlling the nation's majority black population. Mearsheimer's and Walt's use of the term is itself an emotional red herring, certain to inflame opinion against Israel by associating it with one of the most widely hated regimes of the postwar period—a rhetorical trick that I'll discuss in much more detail later in this book when I consider its use by another author, former president Jimmy Carter.

As for the historical accuracy of the claim: Not only do Mearsheimer and Walt select the most extreme negative depiction of what happened at Camp David, but they ignore the further concessions made by Israel in the negotiations at Taba, Egypt, several months after the violence of the second Intifada began. This, too, will be examined in more detail in a later chapter, when I consider how Jimmy Carter has similarly distorted the historical record concerning the negotiations of 2000–2001.

On terrorism, Mearsheimer and Walt adopt a similarly unbalanced perspective. They concede that the murder of civilians is a bad thing—how could they not? But they minimize the seriousness of the problem of terrorism against Israel by Arabs and specifically by Palestinians, devoting far less space and expressing far less outrage over suicide bombings and similar events than they do over allegations of abuse by Israel.

What's more, they rationalize and defend the practice of terrorism on the ground that "the Palestinians believe they have no other way to force Israeli concessions." Palestinian terrorism, they imply, is really a form of self-defense: "it is largely a response to Israel's prolonged campaign to colonize the West Bank and Gaza Strip."[9]

Most Americans and Israelis see the war on terror as a geopolitical reality that has forced their two nations closer together. After all, both countries have been targeted by some of the same groups, both are denounced by supporters of the same worldview (Islamist), and both are regarded as obstacles to the realization of the jihadists' vision of a purely Islamic Middle East ruled by *sharia* law. But for Mearsheimer and Walt, this seemingly clear strategic bond between the two countries is an illusion:

> . . . the U.S. has a terrorism problem in good part because it is so closely allied with Israel, not the other way around. U.S. support for Israel is not the only source of anti-American terrorism, but it is an important one, and it makes winning the war on terror more difficult. There is no question, for example, that many al Qaeda leaders, including bin Laden, are

motivated by Israel's presence in Jerusalem and the plight of the Palestinians. . . . unconditional support for Israel makes it easier for extremists to rally popular support and to attract recruits.[10]

Mearsheimer and Walt are careful to hedge these statements with qualifiers: "in good part," "not the only source . . . but . . . an important one," and so on. But the overwhelming impression they create is clear: If only the U.S. would dump its undeserving ally, Israel, the terrorists would stop targeting America.

The facts say otherwise. If Islamist anti-Semitic hatred is focused mainly or even largely on the conflict between the Palestinians and Israelis, how can we explain its prevalence among Islamic communities that are very distant from the Middle East and almost entirely uninvolved with that conflict? I'm thinking, for example, of Malaysia, whose prime minister, Mahathir bin Mohamad, notoriously declared, at a 2003 Islamic leadership conference in Putrajaya, Malaysia, that "The Europeans killed 6 million Jews out of 12 million. But today the Jews rule this world by proxy. They get others to fight and die for them."[11] Or of Indonesia, where, according to a survey conducted by the Pew Global Attitudes Project, fully 76 percent of the (mostly Islamic) population openly admit that they have an "unfavorable" view of Jews.[12] Or of Pakistan, where the BBC has reported that sizable numbers of highly educated people are convinced that the 9/11 attacks were planned by "the Jews" and carried out by Israel's Mossad as part of a plot to discredit Islam.[13]

Or, if we want to focus specifically on terrorist violence, how do Mearsheimer and Walt relate the Palestinian issue to Islamist violence in Tunisia (1,400 miles from the territories), where, in April 2002, nineteen people were killed in a bombing at the ancient Ghriba synagogue, an attack for which al-Qaeda later claimed responsibility?[14] What about the Islamist attacks in Bali (in October 2002), Moscow (October 2002), Madrid (March 2004), Beslan, Russia (September 2004), and London (July 2005)? Are Muslims in all these countries motivated primarily or even to any significant extent by concern over the rights of Palestinians? Not even the attackers themselves make any such claim.

The Mearsheimer and Walt theory that Israeli misdeeds in the Palestinian territories are at the root of Islamist terrorism simply isn't supported by the facts. Consider what a long-time student of the region, Martin Kramer of the Washington Institute for Near East Policy, has written about this question:

> Then there is the argument that American support for Israel is the source of popular resentment, propelling recruits to al Qaeda. I do not know of any unbiased terrorism expert who subscribes to this notion. Israel has been around for almost 60 years, and it has always faced terrorism. But never has a terror group emerged that is devoted solely or even primarily to attacking the United States for its support of Israel. Terrorists devoted to killing Americans emerged only after the United States began to enlarge its own military footprint in the Gulf. Al Qaeda emerged from the American deployment in Saudi Arabia. And even when al Qaeda and its affiliates mention

Palestine as a grievance, it is as one grievance among many, the other grievances being American support for authoritarian Arab regimes and now the American presence in Iraq.[15]

As an American, I can say that I would dearly love it if there were some easy and morally cost-free way for us to stop being targets of Islamist terrorism. Unfortunately, there is not—and certainly abandoning our friendship with Israel wouldn't achieve that goal.

All of Mearsheimer and Walt's blame-casting and aspersions against Israel serve to set up their main purpose: the demonization of what they describe as the "Israel Lobby." Since Israel is now established as the bad guy, as not serving American interests, the activities of the Lobby are by definition working against what is good for America. The use of the definite article and the capital letter L—the Lobby—create the impression that this lobby has some clear, unified existence, that it consists of a collection of people and organizations working together in a coordinated fashion toward the same end. It's a convenient stylistic device for the authors, but it's even more effective as a rhetorical trick, implying a far greater degree of unity and control on the part of a small group of Jewish community leaders than the authors can actually demonstrate.

Of course, the fact that there is a lobby (lower-case L) made up of Americans who believe that U.S. interests are best served by a strong alliance with Israel is obvious and non-controversial. The American Israel Public Affairs Committee (AIPAC) bills itself as "America's Pro-Israel Lobby." It is registered as a domestic lobby, is supported by donations from over 100,000 individual members, and receives no financial backing from Israel or any other foreign entity. There is nothing unusual about this. Spend ten minutes on Google and you can easily find similar advocacy groups that represent the interests of Irish Americans, Mexican Americans, Indian Americans, Italian Americans, and practically every other imaginable ethnic and national group in the United States. Only the American lobby for Israel seems to be subject to such intense critical scrutiny and even demonization by people like Mearsheimer and Walt.

The authors recognize that they are on shaky ground here. They acknowledge that, in a democratic America, pro-Israel activists have every right to lobby their government. They are also careful to state that they are not suggesting any conspiracy by Jews aimed at world domination, like that depicted by the notorious anti-Semitic forgery *The Protocols of the Elders of Zion.* Mearsheimer and Walt clearly regard themselves not as bigoted but as serious scholars attempting to make a responsible argument.

But their claims of even-handedness and objectivity, in the end, are merely lip service, because of the nonstop one-sidedness of their presentation, their gross exaggeration of the power of the lobby, their disregard for the consistently broad-based American public support for Israel, their omission of the very many interests that the U.S. has in a strong and safe Israel, and their overriding theme that policy-makers are controlled by the lobby. No matter how the authors protest, all of this adds up to an effort to delegitimize the work of pro-Israel activists.

In this way, the Mearsheimer and Walt article has many of the elements that are familiar from the classic anti-Jewish conspiracy theories throughout history. Visit any anti-Semitic website, read any anti-Semitic tract, attend any meeting by a hate group that targets Jews, and you'll hear the same old themes: the Jews have too much power; they are more loyal to "their own kind" and to the State of Israel than they are to their native country; they exercise political influence not as individual citizens but as a cabal, working together behind the scenes to force non-Jews to do their bidding. Walt and Mearsheimer sound all the same notes—not with the crudity we'd encounter from spokespeople for neo-Nazi groups like the National Alliance, but with a subtlety and pseudoscholarly style that makes their poison all the more dangerous.

In order to justify their accusations, Mearsheimer and Walt deliberately distort basic realities. For example, they try to make the case that the Lobby stifles any discussions that might lead to criticism of Israel, and they have searched diligently for evidence to prove this point. Apparently the evidence was hard to come by, since even the examples they cite tend to *undermine* rather than prove their case.

Here are a couple of examples. Mearsheimer and Walt write:

> There is . . . a strong norm [among Jewish leaders] against criticizing Israeli policy, and Jewish-American leaders rarely support putting pressure on Israel. Thus, Edgar Bronfman Sr., the president of the World Jewish Congress, was accused of "perfidy" when he wrote a letter to President Bush in mid-2003 urging him to persuade Israel to curb construction of its

controversial "security fence." Critics declared that "it would be obscene at any time for the president of the World Jewish Congress to lobby the president of the United States to resist policies being promoted by the government of Israel."[16]

Let's put aside Mearsheimer's and Walt's tendentious summary of this incident, which implies that it demonstrates the "strong norm against criticizing Israeli policy," and consider *what actually happened.* The president of a leading Jewish organization (actually a federation of international Jewish communities and organizations) *did in fact criticize* Israeli policy—and in a letter to the president of the United States no less. He was then subsequently criticized for his action by another Jewish leader who disagreed with him. Does this illustrate lock-step conformity among Jewish leaders or healthy, open disagreement? I'd say the latter.

Here is the second example Mearsheimer and Walt use to try to prove their point:

> Similarly, when Israel Policy Forum president Seymour Reich advised Secretary of State Condoleezza Rice to pressure Israel to reopen a critical border crossing in the Gaza Strip in November 2005, critics denounced his action as "irresponsible behavior," and declared that, "There is absolutely no room in the Jewish mainstream for actively canvassing against the security-related policies . . . of Israel."[17]

Once again, a Jewish leader criticizes Israel publicly; then another Jewish leader disagrees with him, equally publicly. These stories are supposed to demonstrate how the Lobby enforces rigid ideological conformity when it comes to Israel? Some conformity! Not only can't the Lobby control the rest of America—apparently, it can't even control its own leadership.

When Mearsheimer and Walt try to show the overwhelming power of the Lobby to control political debate about Israel, they focus on the U.S. Congress. From a rhetorical point of view, that's not surprising. There is, in fact, a high degree of support for the State of Israel and for some (though not all) Israeli policies in the halls of Congress among both Democratic and Republican lawmakers. This state of affairs might give the impression that "Jewish control" is a reality.

However, when we look more closely at the evidence that Mearsheimer and Walt adduce to try to prove that Congress supports Israel purely because of the political clout of the Lobby, it is surprisingly weak. For instance, here is the sole example they offer of a member of Congress whom the Lobby successfully "punished" for ideological impurity:

> There is no doubt about the potency of these tactics [i.e., AIPAC's attempts to influence election campaigns]. To take but one example, in 1984 AIPAC helped defeat Senator Charles Percy from Illinois, who, according to a prominent Lobby figure, had "displayed insensitivity and even hostility to our concerns." Thomas Dine, the head of AIPAC at the time, explained what happened: "All the Jews in America, from coast to coast, gathered to oust Percy. And the American politicians—those who hold public positions now, and those who aspire—got the message."[18]

Let's ignore the fact that, in the aftermath of the 1984 election, both Edward Vrdolyak and Harold Washington—two leading Illinois politicians—attributed Percy's defeat neither to Jewish pressure nor even to defections by Jewish voters but to the fact that the Chicago Democratic Party had done an usually good job of mobilizing African American voters in support of their candidate, Paul Simon.[19] Instead, let's focus on how lame this example is. One would think, from the way Mearsheimer and Walt describe it, that the Lobby claims congressional scalps on a regular basis, defeating disliked candidates and elevating favored ones in every election cycle. Yet the authors apparently have to go back *over twenty years* to find a single, somewhat dubious illustration of the Lobby's supposedly tyrannical power.

Impressive? No, not very.

By the way, Mearsheimer's and Walt's failure to mount a convincing case on this front is not solely due to their lack of diligence or research skills. Michael Massing's largely supportive follow-up article in the *New York Review of Books* included a paragraph in which he alluded to "several politicians who had suffered because they had offended AIPAC":

> They include Tony Beilenson in Los Angeles (because he had wanted to divert one percent of all U.S. foreign aid—including aid to Israel—to help drought victims in sub-Saharan Africa); John Bryant of Texas (for seeking to withhold funds in order to protest Israel's settlements policy); and James Moran of Virginia, who found that his anticipated election funds dropped several tens of thousands of dollars after he

said at a town meeting in 2003 that the Iraq war would not have been fought had it not been for the strong support of the Jewish community.

So Massing's "several politicians" actually amount to only three—Beilenson, Bryant, and Moran. At least Massing was able to come up with three recent cases, not just a single warmed-over example from twenty years ago. But here is the kicker. His account of the electoral onslaught by AIPAC ends with the following sentence, complete with sheepish parentheses: "(Both Bryant and Moran won anyway.)" [20]

So in the end, *a single congressman* allegedly targeted by AIPAC was actually defeated—and whether or not AIPAC's involvement played a decisive role in the election result is, of course, impossible to determine with certainty.

The all-powerful Lobby doesn't look like much of a steamroller, does it?

Similarly, the authors' claim that the Lobby prevents appointments in the executive branch of government of anyone critical of Israel is absurd. Naturally, friends of Israel hope to have friends in every administration, but to conclude that they in any way control this process ignores a range of officials who have served in recent administrations, ranging from Zbigniew Brzezinski and James Baker to Brent Scowcroft and Colin Powell, as well as many, many others, whom no one would describe as being "in Israel's pocket."

Mearsheimer's and Walt's tendentious game grows even weaker when they try to make the same point with regard to two other U.S.

institutions, the media and university campuses. To suggest that criticism of Israel in these two places is stifled is laughable. The list of critics of Israel both in the media and in academia is lengthy, and attacks on Zionism that sometimes border on the anti-Semitic are commonplace on campuses.

Mearsheimer and Walt can't resist toying with the notion that individuals with a pro-Israel agenda dominate the news media and manipulate its coverage to their advantage. The belief that Jews secretly control the mainstream press and use it as a medium for insidious propaganda has long been a staple of anti-Semitic fantasy. The mythical Learned Elders of Zion themselves boast of their power over the media in "Protocol Number 2": "Through the Press we have gained the power to influence while remaining ourselves in the shade."[21] And the same imaginary power was a constant theme of Henry Ford's rabidly anti-Semitic newspaper, the *Dearborn Independent.*

Mearsheimer and Walt are not rabble-rousers on a par with Henry Ford, and their essay is far less blatant than the *Protocols.* They feel at least a modicum of compunction to offer evidence, however sketchy, to back up their claims. Here is how they try to convict the nation's leading newspaper, the *New York Times,* of pro-Israel bias:

> The *Times* occasionally criticizes Israeli policies and sometimes concedes that the Palestinians have legitimate grievances, but it is not even-handed. In his memoirs, for example, former *Times* executive editor Max Frankel acknowledged the impact his own pro-Israel attitude had on his editorial choices. In his words: "I was much more deeply devoted to Is-

rael than I dared to assert." He goes on: "Fortified by my knowledge of Israel and my friendships there, I myself wrote most of our Middle East commentaries. As more Arab than Jewish readers recognized, I wrote them from a pro-Israel perspective."[22]

Perhaps without even realizing it, Mearsheimer and Walt are, of course, conflating two different things: the personal attitude of an individual who worked for the *Times* and the actual nature of the reporting, commentary, and editorial choices reflected on the pages of the newspaper. The two may often be very different and even dramatically opposed, as we saw earlier in this book when we considered how the *Times* itself covered the explosive story of the Holocaust.

Even Frankel's own words, as quoted by Mearsheimer and Walt, undermine their point. Frankel tells us that he did not "dare to assert" his devotion to Israel, and that "more Arab than Jewish readers recognized" his pro-Israel perspective. Is this the tone of a person who is using the power of America's greatest newspaper to spread propaganda on behalf of a favored cause? Doesn't it, rather, sound like someone who bent over backward to *conceal* his personal attitude so as not to alienate readers or lose their trust? And exactly how biased could Frankel's commentaries have been if, in his own words, relatively few Jewish readers even *noticed* his pro-Israel bent?

The fact is that the *Times,* like virtually all of the mainstream media, works hard to be even-handed in its coverage of Israel and the Middle East—so much so that pro-Israel organizations like CAMERA (the Committee for Accuracy in Middle East Reporting in America) and individual commentators such as Ed Lasky, of the conservative blog American Thinker, actually accuse the *Times* of anti-Israel bias bordering on the anti-Semitic! (You may or may not agree with the conclusions reached by a writer like Lasky, but if you read the articles in which he presents his arguments, you'll at least discover that he has marshaled far more factual evidence than Mearsheimer and Walt have bothered to amass on behalf of their opposing viewpoint.)[23]

As evidence of the power of the Lobby over academia, Mearsheimer and Walt cite the establishment of endowed chairs and programs in Jewish studies in universities around the country. Aside from the fact that the authors simply ignore the importance of such scholarship to society and the Jewish community, to speak of this as an indicator of Jewish power without a mention of the millions of dollars being spent by the Persian Gulf's Arab regimes to set up massive programs at major universities is just one more example of how outlandish their work is.

Perhaps most shockingly, Mearsheimer and Walt actually contradict their own pious disclaimers about the right of any group—including American Jews and supporters of Israel—to publicly advocate on behalf of favored causes when they write, in the very first endnote to their paper, the following amazing sentences:

> Indeed, the mere existence of the Lobby suggests that unconditional support for Israel is not in the American national interest. If it was, one would not need an organized special interest group to bring it about. But because Israel is a strate-

gic and moral liability, it takes relentless political pressure to keep U.S. support intact.[24]

Think for a moment about the logic implied here. If we take Mearsheimer and Walt at their word, any cause that is supported by "an organized special interest group" is thereby exposed as being "not in the American national interest." After all, according to the authors, any policy that *is* in the national interest will fall into place naturally and automatically, with no need for public advocacy! This is a stunningly naïve view of how government works. It also, at a stroke, condemns the efforts of any "organized special interest group" in America as being, ipso facto, opposed to the national interest—a revelation that might startle and dismay the members of AARP, the NAACP, the labor unions, the Chamber of Commerce, NOW, the Audubon Society, the American Legion, the Consumers Union . . . name your favorite cause. Mearsheimer and Walt have declared them all out-of-bounds!

Actually, I don't believe for a second that the authors really mean what they say. Their animus is clearly directed at one and only one interest group in America—namely, the fearsome Israel lobby. The fact that two respected scholars could stumble into making a broad statement as inane as this one only suggests the depth of the irrationality to which their resentment of the lobby has driven them. No one with any real confidence in the strength of their arguments would find it necessary to resort to such exaggerations as this one.

As to anti-Semitism in Europe, which is depicted as another subject that the Lobby manipulates to gain power and influence, Mearsheimer and Walt do the expected: They accuse the Jews of falsely screaming anti-Semitism at what they suggest is merely legitimate criticism of Israel. The fact that European leaders like Jacques Chirac, Silvio Berlusconi, and Joschka Fischer long ago made clear that there is a serious problem of anti-Semitism makes no impression on the authors. Nor do they recognize that so many in the Jewish community clearly differentiate between legitimate criticism of the Jewish State and the demonization, delegitimization, and double standard employed against Israel that is either inherently anti-Semitic or generates an environment of anti-Semitism.

Finally, three quarters of the way through the text of the article, Mearsheimer and Walt turn to their most timely and controversial topic: the Bush administration's decision to invade Iraq. Here, one suspects, is the real driving force behind the article. As we've seen, by the time the article appeared, in the spring of 2006, the insurgency in Iraq had proven more resilient and dangerous than administration officials and their supporters had anticipated. The war was turning out to be more costly, both in treasure and in American lives, than Bush and his team had promised, and the results on the ground were disappointing. The fledgling Iraqi democracy was struggling to establish itself, and the country was teetering on the brink of full-fledged civil war. For all these reasons, public opinion was turning against the war, a shift that would be dramatically underscored by the Democratic takeover of the House and Senate in the fall midterm elections.

Here, then, is the United States embroiled in an unpopular war that is unfolding unhappily. There obviously is much room for criticism, including criticism of the so-called neoconservative advisors, pundits, academics, and journalists who supported the original decision to go to war. And many writers and politicians have stepped forward in the last couple of years to voice those criticisms and to call for changes in U.S. foreign policy going forward. All of this is part of the healthy debate on which democracy thrives.

But Mearsheimer and Walt approach the topic of Iraq with a very different agenda. Their goal is to identify and target a scapegoat for what they consider the mistaken decision to invade Iraq. And that scapegoat, unsurprisingly, is the Lobby, which, according to Mearsheimer and Walt, drove America into war not to serve the best interests of the United States but to serve their *true* homeland, Israel. In their words:

> Pressure from Israel and the Lobby was not the only factor behind the decision to attack Iraq in March 2003, but it was a critical element. . . . Within the United States, the main driving force behind the war was a small band of neo-conservatives, many with close ties to Israel's Likud Party. In addition, key leaders of the Lobby's major organizations lent their voices to the campaign for war.[25]

Here is the subtext of the entire article—the grand syllogism to which Mearsheimer's and Walt's disjointed argument has been pointing: The neocons got us into Iraq; many of the neocons are members of or supporters of the Lobby; many of the neocons are Jewish and have "ties" to Israel; therefore, the war can be blamed on the Lobby.

The desire to find someone to blame for an unfolding American misfortune is understandable. Once again, however, the logic and factual accuracy of Mearsheimer's and Walt's analysis leave much to be desired.

The neoconservatives, whom Mearsheimer and Walt discuss as if they were a tightly knit, monolithic group, are in fact a loosely defined collection of intellectuals from various walks of life—academia, think tanks, government policy posts, journalism—who generally share a view that the United States should take a forceful stance in international affairs. Some happen to be Jewish, some are not; some consider the alliance between the United States and Israel a cornerstone of American strategy, others lay less stress upon it. However, whether one agrees with their views or not, there is no basis for suggesting that Israel's interests supersede those of the United States in their thinking. Nor does the evidence suggest that the neocons have in fact wielded a controlling influence over U.S. foreign policy at any time during their existence as a definable intellectual presence.

As in other parts of their paper, Mearsheimer and Walt unwittingly reveal much of the weakness of their own argument. For example, their thesis holds that the Lobby has been a dominant influence on U.S. foreign policy for decades, and they specifically mention the neocons as having wielded enormous power starting in the Reagan ad-

ministration. Nonetheless, here is the history they are forced to acknowledge:

> Pro-Israel forces have long been interested in getting the U.S.
> military more directly involved in the Middle East, so it could
> help protect Israel. But they had limited success on this front
> during the Cold War, because America acted as an "off-shore
> balancer" in the region. Most U.S. forces designated for the
> Middle East, like the Rapid Deployment Force, were kept
> "over the horizon" and out of harm's way. Washington main-
> tained a favorable balance of power by playing local powers
> off against each other, which is why the Reagan administra-
> tion supported Saddam [Hussein] against revolutionary Iran
> during the Iran-Iraq War (1980–88).[26]

According to Mearsheimer and Walt, the all-powerful Lobby and
its neocon allies wanted American soldiers on the ground in the Middle East. They also wanted the United States to take the lead in defending Israel against potential adversaries in the region, including both
Iraq and Iran. Yet somehow—inexplicably, according to the
Mearsheimer-Walt theory of neocon omnipotence—the Reagan administration followed a very different policy. It kept U.S. forces out of
harm's way and actually supported Saddam Hussein's Iraq.

Later, during the first Bush administration, many of the neocons
urged that the first Gulf War be prosecuted more aggressively. They
wanted coalition forces not simply to drive Iraq out of Kuwait but also
to topple Saddam Hussein from power. Once again, the United States
chose to follow a different policy, leaving Hussein's regime intact and

even failing to honor an implied promise to support the Kurds in northern Iraq should they rebel against the government in Baghdad. Again, the supposedly dominant clique of neocon-Lobby insiders were inexplicably thwarted. (Mearsheimer and Walt don't discuss this episode, perhaps because, like so many other elements of Middle Eastern history, it doesn't fit comfortably into their thesis.)

As time passed, the desire of the neocons and the Lobby to launch an attack on Iraq persisted. Here is how Mearsheimer and Walt describe their attempts to drive U.S. policy in the late 1990s and early 2000s:

> The neoconservatives were already determined to topple Saddam before [George W.] Bush became President. They caused a stir in early 1998 by publishing two open letters to President Clinton calling for Saddam's removal from power. The signatories, many of whom had close ties to pro-Israel groups like JINSA or WINEP, and whose ranks included Elliot Abrams, John Bolton, Douglas Feith, William Kristol, Bernard Lewis, Donald Rumsfeld, Richard Perle and Paul Wolfowitz, had little trouble convincing the Clinton Administration to adopt the general goal of ousting Saddam. But the neoconservatives were unable to sell a war to achieve that objective. Nor were they able to generate much enthusiasm for invading Iraq in the early months of the Bush Administration. As important as the neoconservatives were for making the Iraq war happen, they needed help to achieve their aim.
>
> That help arrived with 9/11. Specifically, the events of that day led Bush and Cheney to reverse course and become strong proponents of a preventive war to topple Saddam.[27]

Again, let's try to ignore Mearsheimer and Walt's tendentious rhetoric, including the roll call of largely Jewish-sounding neocon names, and focus on the *actual events* the authors recount. The neocons spent years vigorously advocating an attack on Iraq—and they got nowhere. Neither a Democratic administration nor a Republican one was willing to adopt their proposals, not even a Republican administration that had hired some of their number in key policymaking positions. Only after the world-changing events of September 11, 2001, did the administration's key policymakers—non-Jewish, non-Lobby members named George Bush, Dick Cheney, Donald Rumsfeld, Condoleezza Rice, and Colin Powell—decide that an attack on Iraq was the best course for the United States.

I wonder if someone can explain to me how this sequence of events demonstrates the decisive, unprecedented, disturbing power of the Lobby and the neocons in determining U.S. policy?

Today there's the issue of Iran developing nuclear capability. In this matter, as in everything else, Mearsheimer and Walt assume that it is Israel's alleged interests that drive U.S. policy. Again, reality doesn't support their thesis.

The authors make much of the fact that certain specific neocons have advocated a hard line on Iran—just as Israel's prime minister Ariel Sharon had done. Aha!—Proof that the Israeli agenda is in control. This might be convincing if Israel alone were concerned about the threat posed by a nuclear Iran. Yet, not only Israel and the United States, but the UN's Security Council, the International Atomic Energy

Agency, and even the countries of Western Europe (where, as Mearsheimer and Walt acknowledge, the power of the Lobby is minimal) see Iran's nuclear aspirations as a threat to world peace.

In March 2007—just a few days ago, as I write this chapter—Russia reportedly announced that it would be withholding promised deliveries of nuclear fuel for Tehran's first atomic power plant. Russia's decision is motivated in part by worries over Iran's nuclear intentions.

All these facts seem to be lost on Mearsheimer and Walt. Perhaps that's just as well; otherwise, they might be led to conclude that the Israel lobby now controls not just the U.S. Congress but also the United Nations, Western Europe, and even the Kremlin under Vladimir Putin!

I feel as though I am verging on overkill, that perhaps I've offered enough examples of the credibility problems embodied in Mearsheimer's and Walt's paper to enable you to draw your own conclusions. Let me be sure my point is clear: A factual error or misinterpretation here and there in a scholarly paper is not a big problem. None of us is perfect. But when a much-acclaimed and widely read paper by two distinguished academic authors is *riddled* with errors, and when all of those errors tend to slant the paper *in the exact same direction,* we are dealing not with a little unfortunate carelessness but with a culpable degree of bias. The examples that I've been at pains to document all point to the authors' relentless obsession to see the world through their own narrowly conceived and distorted prism, one that makes Israel and its American allies in the so-called Lobby into the source of most of the evils haunting the international scene today.

The result is one of the most unprofessional works of scholarship ever to emanate from supposedly respectable quarters. Undoubtedly, the anti-Israel forces and the avowed bigots will be citing Mearsheimer and Walt for a long time to come.

This use of their theory has already begun. For example, David Duke, the notorious anti-Semite, racist, and former Grand Wizard of the Knights of the Ku Klux Klan, was quick to endorse and praise Mearsheimer and Walt. Duke wrote:

> I have read about the report and read one summary already, and I am surprised how excellent it is. It is quite satisfying to see a body in the premier American university essentially come out and validate every major point I have been making since before the war [in Iraq] even started. . . . the task before us is to wrest control of America's foreign policy and critical junctures of media from the Jewish extremist neocons that seek to lead us into what they expectantly call World War Four.[28]

I don't believe in guilt by association. I understand that Mearsheimer and Walt can't be held responsible for every individual who chooses to praise their work. (Hitler was a vegetarian, and if Hitler were to praise a vegetarian tract, it would be unfair to criticize its author on that score.) What's disturbing is that "The Israel Lobby" does in fact espouse arguments and beliefs that are very closely aligned to those held by anti-Semites and racists of the David Duke variety. Either explicitly or by implication, the article embraces half a dozen of the most common and poisonous assertions that anti-Semites have long peddled: that Jews are treacherous practitioners of "dual loyalty" who are ready to sell out America for their selfish interests; that Jews cooperate behind the scenes to manipulate national institutions for their own benefit; that Jews wield a disproportionate amount of economic and political power; and that they control, or try to control, the press, the media, and the universities so as to stifle dissent and prevent the world from understanding their true objectives.

These are bigoted canards of great antiquity. Those who believe them—like David Duke—are out of touch with reality and would be highly dangerous in any position of power. By promoting these beliefs and giving them a veneer of academic respectability, Mearsheimer and Walt are playing into the hands of the David Dukes of the world. And it is not an accusation of guilt by association to say so.

We can only hope that well-intentioned people will see "The Israel Lobby" for what it is—a classic conspiratorial analysis invoking the canards of "Jewish power," "Jewish self-interest," and "Jewish control," thereby feeding and strengthening the false—and deadly—beliefs that foster anti-Semitism both in America and around the world. Sadly, the positive response that Mearsheimer and Walt have received—and not just from the David Dukes of the world—is a testimony, if any were needed, to the enduring appeal of anti-Semitic stereotypes and falsehoods in a troubled time when too many people are seeking the security and simplicity of scapegoating.

We can't turn back the clock to an easier, more peaceful time. The terrible events of 9/11 happened, and they can't be undone. Neither can the invasion of Iraq or the painful, ongoing struggle for mutual understanding and peaceful coexistence in the Middle East. It's our responsibility to wrestle with these challenges and find honorable responses to them. In that effort, vigorous and open debate is essential—but demonizing our opponents, as Mearsheimer and Walt too often do, will only weaken our democracy, not strengthen it.

———————◆———————

As I was completing work on this chapter, Mearsheimer and Walt published a 32-page document that they billed as a rebuttal of the many criticisms their original essay "The Israel Lobby" had received. The venue was the Spring 2007 issue of a newsletter titled *America and the Future,* and they called their rebuttal "Setting the Record Straight: A Response to Critics of 'The Israel Lobby.'" A more apt title might have been, "We Were Right the First Time."

It would truly be overkill to devote the time and space to a complete dissection of the further distortions and logical errors committed by Mearsheimer and Walt in this new article. It would also be very repetitious, since much of "Setting the Record Straight" consists of simple denials that the original essay contains the tendentious and biased ideas that so many critics have found in it, accompanied by lengthy quotations from the essay that the authors think exonerate them. In most cases, this means that the so-called response is simply a rehash of the authors' original essay, not a substantive clarification or defense at all.

For example, in response to the charge that Mearsheimer and Walt "portray the Israel lobby as a Jewish conspiracy or cabal," the authors merely assert that this was not their intention and quote a long paragraph from their essay in which they explicitly disavow it. They conclude, "Thus, the charge that we portray the lobby as a conspiracy or cabal is not correct, and those who have made this accusation either have not read our article carefully or have misrepresented what we actually wrote."[29]

Of course, this "response" is not nearly as conclusive as the authors seem to believe. They might have asked themselves, "Given the fact that our original essay explicitly stated that we do not consider the Israel lobby to be a conspiracy or cabal, why did so many readers of the essay conclude that we believe exactly that?" The answer is very simple: Page after page of "The Israel Lobby" is filled with assertions, anecdotes, accusations, and claims that, taken together, either explicitly state or clearly imply that American supporters of Israel work together in a coordinated fashion to distort the nation's foreign policy on behalf of illegitimate goals (namely, the enhancement and expansion of Israeli power in the Middle East) that the majority of Americans would not support if they fully understood them; to control the U.S. government in the pursuit of those goals; and to suppress any dissent or attempt to challenge their policy positions, not through fair and open debate, but through the use of political power to intimidate and silence opponents.

This clearly and unmistakably describes a conspiracy or cabal. The mere fact that the authors don't use the word "conspiracy" or "cabal," and that they even take the trouble to write a few sentences claiming that they are *not* describing a conspiracy or cabal, doesn't change the fact that that is what they are describing! For Mearsheimer and Walt to disavow the clear message of their entire essay by pointing to a paragraph or two that deny the obvious is, at best, highly disingenuous.

When it comes to defending the detailed factual underpinnings of their essay, Mearsheimer and Walt engage in question-begging, equivocation, and other forms of dubious logic. For example, they devote several pages to challenging historian Benny Morris's scathing attack on their work, citing their own analysis of Morris's distinguished historical writings in their defense—as though Mearsheimer and Walt are better qualified to interpret Morris's scholarship than is Morris himself.

They also try to cover up some of their factual errors by subtly and covertly shifting the terms of the debate. For example, consider this point, which the authors appear to consider quite telling:

> Morris's claim that the Second Intifada "was launched by the Palestinians" also does not stand up against the evidence. There is no evidence that Arafat started the Second Intifada.[30]

In this paragraph, Mearsheimer and Walt are treating "the Palestinians" as synonymous with "Arafat." Obviously an assertion that the

Second Intifada began with an outbreak of Palestinian violence is *not* tantamount to claiming that Yasser Arafat personally issued some sort of order to make the violence happen. The Mearsheimer and Walt "rebuttal" refutes a claim that Morris did not make—a bit of rhetorical sleight of hand that the authors are evidently hoping their readers will not notice.

As in their original essay, Mearsheimer and Walt are happy to employ a double standard in judging Israel and other nations when it will help them bolster their case. For example, in an attempt to strengthen their assertions about the moral culpability of Israel in connection with the wars of 1948, 1967, and 1973, they seek to deny a point made by one of their most prominent and vocal critics, Harvard law professor and prolific author Alan Dershowitz:

> Contrary to what Dershowitz says, the Arabs were not trying to "drive the Jews into the Sea" in any of those three wars. . . . There is no question that some Arab leaders *talked* about "driving the Jews into the Sea" during the 1948 war, but this was mainly rhetoric designed to appease their publics. In fact, the Arab leaders were mainly concerned about gaining territory for themselves at the expense of the Palestinians.[31]

I'll pass over the interesting point in the last sentence, which seems to drastically undermine a couple of Mearsheimer and Walt's central themes: that the sufferings of the Palestinians are almost entirely due to the crimes of the Israelis, and that the entire Arab world has long been deeply and sincerely concerned about the fate of the Palestinians and hostile to Israel mainly because of this sympathy.

Instead, notice how the authors deal with the inconvenient fact that Arab leaders did in fact claim precisely the goal Dershowitz attributed to them—namely, to "drive the Jews into the Sea." They dismiss this as mere "rhetoric" driven by politics and therefore meaningless. Fascinating—and rather bizarre. Throughout "The Israel Lobby," Mearsheimer and Walt quote with glee the most extreme and incriminating-sounding statements from Israeli leaders about their intention to control lands in Palestine—often, as we've seen, out of context. They don't hesitate to take these statements at face value and to condemn Israel on that basis. But evidently Arab statements that are far more aggressive and bellicose should be brushed aside with a wave of the hand—mere rhetoric, not to be taken seriously!

Those, like Mearsheimer and Walt, who indignantly deny that anti-Israel critics slant their analyses ought to consider this comparison. It's a textbook example of the double standard at work.

The most important point about Mearsheimer's and Walt's response, however, is the way in which they—again, rather subtly—back away from the impression they created in "The Israel Lobby" of an all-powerful cabal of Jewish organizations bending U.S. policy in their favor. In the months since their essay was published, numerous critics have attacked the factual accuracy of this image and denounced its tendency to reinforce a traditional and pernicious anti-Semitic stereotype. So it's not surprising that Mearsheimer and Walt should quietly retreat from it. Yet even as they do so, they loudly declare that their original position remains unchanged. It's a form of fancy rhetorical footwork they must employ in order to defend the frankly indefensible.

Here's an example. Mearsheimer and Walt acknowledge that David Gergen, who served in presidential administrations of both parties, has disagreed with their characterization of the power of the Israel lobby; they say it is "at variance" with what Gergen personally observed during his years in the Oval Office.[32] Actually, Gergen's language was even stronger than Mearsheimer and Walt suggest. His comments on their thesis included the blanket denial, "Over the course of four tours in the White House, I never once saw a decision in the Oval Office to tilt U.S. foreign policy in favor of Israel at the expense of America's interest."[33]

In an effort to discredit Gergen's testimony, the authors recount an episode from the Reagan administration in which Congress voted to allocate more military assistance to Israel than Reagan and his secretary of state, George Shultz, favored. Based on this anecdote, they conclude, "In short, Secretary Shultz knew from the start that the [Israel] Lobby was a potent force that he had to take into account when formulating U.S. Middle East policy."[34]

Quite a tactical retreat! From crediting the Israel lobby, in their original essay, with the power not only to control U.S. policy but to actually silence and punish any voices raised in opposition to it, now

Mearsheimer and Walt are merely calling it "a potent force" that policy makers need "to take into account."

Of course, when tackling any complex, controversial issue—whether the Middle East, Social Security, tax policy, farm subsidies, or education reform—U.S. administrations know there are usually many "potent forces" that need to be "taken into account" before making a final decision. That's an inherent part of the political process. And Mearsheimer and Walt surely know that to declare the pro-Israel lobby merely one such force in the debate over the Middle East is scarcely newsworthy, let alone controversial and inflammatory. But having made much more sweeping claims in their original paper—and having reaped both a storm of controversy and a publicity windfall as a result—they now quietly retreat to this more defensible position, without admitting any shift.

Similarly, in an effort to defend themselves against the charge that they accused American Jews of "dual loyalty" for their support of Israel, Mearsheimer and Walt now bend over backward to acknowledge the truth "that all Americans have many affinities and commitments—to country, family, church, ethnic groups, etc." They (rightly) go on to add:

> In the United States, it is entirely legitimate for this sort of affinity or attachment to manifest itself in politics. Indeed, it is possible for Americans to hold dual citizenship and to serve in foreign armies, and it is certainly legitimate for Americans to advocate for policies intended in part to benefit a foreign country.[35]

Fine—but then *why write a forty-page article devoted to describing and denouncing behavior you consider commonplace and "entirely legitimate"?* Are Mearsheimer and Walt planning to publish similar essays about the dangers to America posed by "The Cuba Lobby," "The Greek Lobby," "The Catholic Lobby," "The Irish Lobby," or "The Farmers Lobby"? Of course not—because, although Mearsheimer and Walt piously claim they regard all such lobbying efforts as "entirely legitimate," there is just one lobby they fear and abhor—the Israel lobby.

Naturally, the authors would claim they have a good reason for their single-minded concern: namely, the fact that the Israel lobby has, in their view, been successfully advocating policy positions they view as detrimental to America's interests. Obviously, most U.S. policymakers disagree with them on this point, as do a vast majority of American citizens. But Mearsheimer and Walt are, of course, perfectly free to think otherwise.

And they have a simple remedy available to them: Win the policy debate! If Mearsheimer and Walt can propose a new set of Middle East policies that they think will bring peace to the region and protect U.S. interests more effectively than current policies, they should lay out their ideas and present cogent arguments on their behalf. If their arguments are convincing, they will surely attract supporters in the general population, in academic and journalistic circles, and ultimately among elected officials. That is how government policies get changed, and Mearsheimer and Walt should be encouraged to pursue that course.

But they've chosen to do otherwise. They are devoting their considerable talents and their illustrious reputations not to making substantive policy arguments but to complaining about the process and suggesting that their opponents in the policy debate are somehow using unfair tactics to withhold the victory that Mearsheimer and Walt believe they deserve. This is not a positive contribution to the national conversation.

3

ALLURING MYTHS, CLEAR-EYED REALITIES

WE'VE SEEN THAT JOHN MEARSHEIMER'S AND Stephen Walt's essay "The Israel Lobby" is a tissue of half-truths, falsehoods, and innuendos, woven together in a superficially impressive academic style (footnotes and all) in order to suggest a thorough scholarly analysis of a weighty policy issue. In fact, their work serves merely as an attractive new package for disseminating a series of familiar but false beliefs about Jews, Israel, and their relationship to the rest of the world, including specifically the United States of America.

Avowed anti-Semites hold most or all of these beliefs, and many openly promulgate them. Others who are merely bigoted or biased may share some of them, perhaps only semiconsciously. Still others who in most circumstances are neither anti-Semitic nor biased in their beliefs and actions may have some hidden sympathy with these beliefs, which may rise to the surface in times of social or personal stress.

These beliefs are widely appealing because, in one way or another, they all make Israel and the Jews into scapegoats for serious problems faced by the people of the United States and the world. Thus, they deflect attention from errors in judgment, failures of nerve, or moral lapses committed by other nations, groups, or individuals; they minimize the need for serious study of the underlying social, economic, political, and cultural factors that make real-world problem solving difficult; and they offer a convenient emotional outlet for people who enjoy venting their anger or resentment on a group that is too remote, powerless, or abstract to fight back.

In dissecting the Mearsheimer and Walt article, we touched on some of these alluring, tempting, but ultimately groundless beliefs. Now let's delve into them a little more deeply and explicitly. They are important and deserve to be debunked because they are so widespread, finding embodiment not only in writings like those of Mearsheimer and Walt but also, more subtly, in other elements of the public discourse—in the sly insinuations of a radio talk-show host, in the nasty caricatures of a crude cartoon, in the subtle accusations hinted at in a campus lecture or even a Sunday sermon. They need to be recognized for what they are: chimeras, phantoms that stand in the way of real understanding of the problems we face, whether as members of particular religious communities or simply as citizens in a complex, diverse world—a world where scapegoating only delays the hard work of finding answers.

The myth: *Israel once "deserved" American support, but it has now become a moral pariah that ought to be shunned and condemned.*

The reality: *Mearsheimer and Walt, like other critics of Israel, are well aware that, for many Americans, Israel's claim to the world's sympathy and support rests partly on a moral basis.*

There are several elements to this moral claim. There is the terrible history of anti-Semitism, primarily in Europe but also in other regions, that drove millions of Jews from their homes and culminated in history's single greatest crime, the Nazi Holocaust. International complicity in that crime leads many people to feel that Israel deserves support as a way of saying to the Jewish people, "We will never again leave you without a home and a safe haven from hatred."

Then there is the fact that Israel is a democratic country, arguably the only true democracy in the Middle East, where the people enjoy the same freedoms for which Americans have fought and died, and where the nation's leaders and its general policies are chosen by the citizens, not by oligarchs, dictators, monarchs or a self-selected elite. The United States has a proud history of serving as the sponsors of democracy around the world; we like to think that we played a crucial role in rescuing freedom during two world wars as well as the twilight struggle of the cold war. In much the same way, we feel drawn to supporting Israel in its quest to maintain democracy in a dangerous part of the world today.

Finally, many Americans feel called to support Israel for reasons of religious sentiment. I'm not referring here to the belief held by many fundamentalist Christians that the re-establishment of the State of Israel is a welcome sign that the end of the world is approaching. Rather, I'm referring to a more general sense of kinship that many American Christians feel with a country that was founded by pilgrims from distant shores, many of them fleeing religious persecution, who viewed their new homeland as a promised land, a gift from God. (This concept of "restorationism," discussed earlier, had much popularity and influence among several generations of Americans.) To this day, many Americans view themselves as spiritual siblings of the Israelis. This is a third strand of feeling that strengthens the sense that Israel has a moral claim to our support.

Yet Mearsheimer and Walt feel strongly that American support for Israel is wrong, and so it is important for them to somehow undermine this claim. In an effort to do this, they devote much time and energy in their essay to cataloging moral misdeeds they attribute to Israel. Some of these are accurate; many are misstated, exaggerated, or simply false. The point they claim to be making—that any view of the Middle East as a battle of "Virtuous Israelis" versus "Evil Arabs" is oversimplified—is probably accurate, as far as it goes.[1] As most people know, life is certainly more complicated than that. But their catalog of Israeli misdeeds begs the crucial question: Is American moral support for Israel predicated on the notion that Israel is a perfect paragon of moral virtue?

For me, the obvious answer is no. If the United States were to seek allies only among nations that exhibit moral perfection, its allies would be few and far between. Is Britain, America's oldest and closest ally, a moral paragon? (Don't ask the people of Northern Ireland that question.) Is France? (The angry Muslim youths who have rioted in the streets of Paris don't seem to think so.) Is Japan? Is Germany? And don't get me started on some of America's other allies in the Middle East, such as Saudi Arabia and Egypt!

Whether or not Israel is a shining moral paragon, it certainly is not a pariah state to be condemned. It is, in fact, a nation among nations—a country much like any other, with its problems, its opportunities, its virtues, and, at times, its failings and shortcomings. In short, Israel is a "normal" country—despite a history that makes it absolutely unique and that does, indeed, exert a moral claim on the decent peoples of the world.

Does this sound contradictory? Maybe so. But this reality of Israel is one that Americans, of all people, are perhaps best positioned to understand.

Like the United States, Israel was founded with idealistic motives. Like many of the early settlers of North America, the Jews who moved to Palestine in the 1930s, '40s, and '50s dreamed of a life of freedom in a new land where they could worship as they pleased, creating prosperity through their own efforts and ingenuity, and living in peace with their neighbors and with all the world. Many of these Jews were socialists, imbued with the high ideals that characterized that movement in the middle of the twentieth century: racial and gender equality, the dignity of labor, human rights, and a decent standard of living for all. Israel, they dreamed, could be more than just a homeland for the Jews, important as that was. It could also be a model of progressive values for the world to admire and emulate.

Today, almost six decades have passed since Israel's founding. The idealism of those golden days has given way to the realism and pragmatism of daily life. This is inevitable. Yet it also brings with it a sense of disillusionment, a loss of innocence. We've experienced this repeatedly in the United States—indeed, it sometimes seems as if every American generation experiences its own loss of innocence somewhere along the way, whether through the assassination of a president, the suffering caused by an unpopular war, or the advent of some terrible and unforeseen disaster. Life itself, with its responsibilities, its hard choices, its setbacks, its mistakes, and its tragedies, has a way of disillusioning everyone in time.

In the case of Israel, the sense that a time of innocence has passed is deeply bound up with the wars that the country has fought and the difficult circumstances those wars have left in their wake.

This is not the place for a recapitulation of Israeli history. Most people reading these pages should know the outlines of the story; some will know it in intimate detail, often from personal experience. Time and again, Israel has been forced to fight against enemies bent on its destruction. Time and again, Israel's armies were equal to the challenge. As a result, since 1967, territories once occupied by Arabs have been under Israeli control and administration. And even today, with (almost) all the world having agreed on the justice of a two-state solution, the fledgling Palestinian state remains a ward of Israel—an unwilling, unwanted, resentful stepchild, seemingly unwilling or unable to govern itself and apparently still prone to lashing out unexpectedly against its baffled parent.

This is a terrible situation for all the parties—for Israel, for the unlucky Palestinians, for neighboring countries like Lebanon and Syria, and for the entire region. People of good will everywhere want it to end, but no one has yet devised a solution and a pathway that everyone is willing to accept and live by.

This sort of history is not conducive to a national sense of idealism or innocence. Wars, even just wars of self-defense, are brutal things. The discipline of having to occupy lands inhabited by poor refugees, many of them hostile to your very existence and some of them willing to commit suicide as the price for killing you, is a harsh and bitter one. Innocent people suffer and die. Decent men and women become hardened, in some cases, brutalized. Momentary passions turn into lasting hatreds and sometimes end up being passed along from one generation to the next.

All of this is part of the tragic legacy of war. And a nation like the United States, whose own historical memories include Wounded Knee, Andersonville, My Lai, and Abu Ghraib, can certainly understand this.

The worst thing that the Arab nations could have done to Israel is what they tried to do—to drive the country and her people into the sea, in a kind of second holocaust. Perhaps the second worst thing that they could have done is what they actually did. They lost their wars against Israel and yet refused to make peace, locking the peoples of the Middle East into a posture of clenched and unremitting hatred from which, at times, it seems there is no escape. How could anyone's innocence survive such an ordeal?

There's no denying that the decades of war and near-war that Israel has suffered have tarnished the nation's moral luster. Israel's treatment of the Palestinians has not been blameless. But, sobering as it is to say, this does not make Israel some kind of pariah. It makes Israel answerable for its actions like every other nation on earth that has had to fight for its own survival and, in the process, has sometimes erred.

Those who want to classify Israel as a pariah state are applying a particularly selective kind of double standard. Here is how historian Walter Laqueur puts it:

> There is a great deal of evil in the world and millions have perished within the last decade or two as the result of civil wars, repression, racial and social persecution, and tribal conflicts, from Cambodia to much of Africa (Congo, Rwanda, and Darfur). More than two billion people live in repressive dictatorships, but there is persecution too in countries that are free or partly free. National and religious minority groups have been systematically persecuted, abused, raped, burned, shot, gassed, and their property demolished, from Indonesia, Pakistan, and Bangladesh, to Central Asia and beyond. In fact, it would be difficult to think of countries outside of Europe and North

America that have been entirely free of such suffering; and even Europe has had such incidents on a massive scale, as in the Balkans. But there have been no protest demonstrations concerning the fate of the Dalets (Untouchables) in India even though there are more than 100 million of them. The fate of the Uighur in China, the Copts in Egypt, or the Bahai in Iran (to name but a few persecuted peoples) has not generated much indignation in the streets of Europe and America.

According to peace researchers, 25 million people were killed in internal conflicts since World War Two, of them, 8,000 in the Israeli-Palestinian conflict, which ranks forty-sixth in the list of victims. But Israel has been more often condemned by the United Nations and other international organizations than all other nations taken together.

. . . Those singling out the Zionist misdeeds certainly do not do so because Israeli injustice has been on a more massive scale. Has criticism of Israel been harsher and so much more frequent simply because better was expected of the Jews? Or was it because Israel was small and isolated and there was prejudice against it?[2]

Don't misunderstand me—I am not saying that Israel should not be held to a high moral standard, or that any mistreatment of Palestinian Arabs that Israel has committed can be excused because "every nation does it." The people of the Book *should* be held to the highest moral standard, and in fact they do so hold themselves, as intense public debate within Israel about the ethical rights and wrongs of the occupation testifies.

What I'm saying is that attempts—like that of Mearsheimer and Walt—to declare Israel unfit to be an American ally because of its so-called moral depredations are hypocritical and slanted. The motivation behind the attempts may not be anti-Semitic, but the inherent bias they embody can't help but nurture the anti-Semitic worldview.

No, Israel may not be perfect. No country is. Does that invalidate Israel's moral claim to the support of the world? I don't think so. If perfection is the standard, all will fall short—including, of course, the United States itself.

The myth: *U.S. support for Israel is disproportionate to the strategic importance of Israel for American interests—which proves that the power of the Israel Lobby is the only possible explanation for that support.*

The reality: *Mearsheimer and Walt claim that Israel is a "strategic liability" to the United States. In their view, the notion that supporting Israel is in America's national interest is absurd. Therefore, they say, some other explanation for the alliance must exist—and they claim to have found it in the supposedly awesome political power of Jewish Americans and the unequaled clout of the Israel Lobby.*

As far as I am concerned—and here I am in agreement with the vast majority of strategic thinkers—Mearsheimer and Walt have it entirely backward. Even if Israel were *not* a Jewish state, and even if Jews were *not* a significant voting bloc in the United States, and even if there *were* no Jewish American lobbying groups supporting Israeli interests—even if all these things were true, supporting Israel would be in the best interests of the United States and would, I believe, be the mainstream policy of both American political parties. Under the circumstances I describe, the U.S.-Israeli alliance would be taken for granted and would be no more controversial than the U.S.-British, U.S.-Mexican, or U.S.-Japanese alliance.

The fact is that there are several important factors that make Israel of strategic importance to the United States. As we've already noted, Israel is the only major democracy in the Middle East. As such, it is a natural ally of America, a country whose values, instincts, policies, and programs all tend to run on parallel lines to our own. In a world where, as many historians and analysts have recently noted, democracies virtually *never* go to war with one another, it only makes sense for two of the world's leading democracies to seek one another out for mutual support. (This is not to say that the United States can enter alliances *only* with democracies; just that an alliance between democracies is inherently attractive, convenient, and sustainable for both parties.)

Second, as a strong military power and a U.S. ally, Israel has proven to be the single greatest source of stability in the region. It is also the chief U.S. proxy and friend in the area, playing a role much like that played by Turkey in Central Asia or Japan in the Far East. Israel has even been described as "an American aircraft carrier" in the Middle East.

Martin Kramer has explained Israel's role as the linchpin of U.S. Middle Eastern policy in a particularly clear and convincing fashion:

American support for Israel—indeed, the illusion of its unconditionality—underpins the Pax Americana in the eastern

Mediterranean. It has compelled Israel's key Arab neighbors to reach peace with Israel and to enter the American orbit. The fact that there has not been a general Arab-Israeli war since 1973 is proof that this Pax Americana, based on the U.S.-Israel alliance, has been a success. From a realist point of view, supporting Israel has been a low-cost way of keeping order in part of the Middle East, managed by the United States from offshore and without the commitment of any force. It is, simply, the ideal realist alliance.[3]

Kramer contrasts the relative stability of Israel's "neighborhood," built around the strong U.S.-Israel alliance, with the instability of the Persian Gulf. At one time, the United States supported the despotic Shah of Iran, but that regional "pillar" collapsed, leaving behind a hostile country that exports terror and harbors territorial designs. Later, the United States supported Saddam Hussein, who ultimately invaded Kuwait, threatened Saudi Arabia, and otherwise destabilized the region. The only possible American response to those crises was to deploy its own forces to restore peace—something that the presence of a powerful Israel makes unnecessary in the eastern Mediterranean region.

Far from being a strategic liability, Israel is a major source of American strength and influence. This is why one American president after another—including both Democrats and Republicans, liberals and conservatives, those inclined toward aggressively interventionist policies and those of an isolationist bent—have all found it in America's interest to support Israel. Even Richard Nixon—who, we now know beyond any reasonable doubt based on recently unearthed historical evidence, was deeply anti-Semitic in his personal beliefs and attitudes[4]—strongly supported the U.S.-Israeli alliance during his presidency. What was true during the cold war is true again in the war against Islamic extremism: The United States, Israel, and the moderate Arab states have common interests in opposing the region's extremist forces. To put it crudely, you don't have to "love the Jews" to see that supporting Israel makes sense for America.

In addition, peace is an American strategic goal, and it is only achievable if Arab states understand that Israel is strong. Egypt and Jordan signed peace treaties with Israel because of Israel's strength, a reality in which American assistance was a significant factor. And if there is hope that others will come round to accepting Israel and ending the conflict, it will be because Israel, backed by the United States, is seen as here to stay and too strong to be attacked.

Add to these geopolitical factors the moral imperative represented by Israel's role as the homeland of the Jewish people, and there's no way to argue convincingly that U.S. support of Israel is "disproportionate" or strategically unsound. Supporting Israel is one area in which doing the right thing is also the smart thing for American interests.

The myth: *U.S. government support for Israel is driven only by the wishes of a vocal, powerful minority.*

The reality: *Anti-Israel critics like to claim, or imply, that American support for Israel does not reflect the will of the people but rather the desire of*

*an elite clique who use their political power, economic clout, and public re-
lations skills to manipulate the government into serving their interests.*

There are two obvious reasons that the critics find this claim attractive. First, it's essential to their mission of delegitimizing support
for Israel. After all, the United States is a democracy, whose govern-
mental leaders proudly insist they follow the expressed will of the voters when setting public policy. While nondemocratic forms of
government might base their claims to legitimacy on guidance from
heaven, a royal prerogative, or "the dynamics of revolution," in a
democracy the preference of a majority is the closest thing we have to
an unshakeable mandate. Thus, if the critics want to convince the
United States to dump Israel from the roll of allies, they must somehow demonstrate that this is what the majority of Americans want—
or, at least, *would* want if they were fully informed.

Second, the notion that U.S. policy toward Israel is driven by an
unrepresentative clique fits beautifully into the traditional anti-
Semitic narrative about "Jewish control." After all, the one unchanging
characteristic of Jews everywhere in the world—with the significant
exception of Israel—is that they are in the minority, and in most
places a tiny minority at that. Therefore, those who hate and fear Jews
must find some way of claiming that the Jews wield power that is disproportionate to their numbers. Hence the popularity of myths about
Jewish cabals, back-room conspiracies involving sinister banking syn-
dicates, secret directives issued by power-mad rabbis—the whole
bizarre rigmarole of paranoid fantasies that finds its classic expression
in the notorious czarist forgery *The Protocols of the Elders of Zion.*

Naturally, scholars like Mearsheimer and Walt don't directly tap into this vein of fantasy. In fact, they explicitly disavow it. But the tenor of their argument, intentionally or not, activates that fantasy and draws upon the emotions it evokes. All they need to do is suggest that the Israel Lobby is a case of the few manipulating the many for their own selfish purposes, and the long history of anti-Jewish slurs centering on conspiracy theories is reborn and immediately leaps into action, whether consciously or not. And here is how Mearsheimer and Walt make this suggestion:

> The United States has a divided government that offers many ways to influence the policy process. As a result, interest groups can shape policy in many different ways—by lobbying elected representatives and members of the executive branch, making campaign contributions, voting in elections, molding public opinion, etc.
>
> Furthermore, special interest groups enjoy *disproportionate power* when they are committed to a particular issue and *the bulk of the population is indifferent.* Policymakers will tend to accommodate those who care about the issue in question, *even if their numbers are small,* confident that the rest of the population will not penalize them.
>
> The Israel Lobby's power flows from its unmatched ability to play this game of interest group politics. [Emphases added.][5]

This might be a fair description of how government policy is shaped in regard to specialized, technical issues like import quotas for particular products or research subsidies for alternative fuels—topics on which a small group of Americans have strong feelings while "the bulk of the population is indifferent." But does it accurately describe the U.S. public's engagement with Israel and the Middle East?

Not at all. The truth is that few issues in American foreign policy show as clear-cut a pattern of public opinion as support for Israel. Solid pluralities of Americans strongly favor the U.S.-Israeli alliance, sympathize primarily with Israel when thinking about the Arab-Israeli and Palestinian-Israeli conflicts, and believe that current U.S. policies toward the Middle East strike approximately the right balance between support for Israel and other interests. What's more, these pluralities have been consistent over time.

Americans are simply *not* "indifferent" to the conflicts in the Middle East. They care a lot about them, and know exactly where they stand—alongside Israel.

Here's how public opinion researchers at the authoritative Pew Research Center summarized their findings on this topic in mid-2006:

> A substantial plurality of the American public has been steadfast in its support for Israel as the intensity of armed conflict in the Middle East has waxed and waned through the years. While Americans have on occasion voiced criticisms of specific tactics and operations undertaken by the Israeli government, their sympathy for the Jewish state has, with only minor variation, remained strong.[6]

Accompanying data show that when Americans are asked, "In the dispute between Israel and the Palestinians, which side do you sympathize with more, Israel or the Palestinians?" the percent responding "Israel" in May 2006 was 48 percent, as compared with just 13 percent that responded "Palestinians." (Eighteen percent responded, "Both" or "Neither," while 21 percent refused to answer or said they didn't know.) Over the years when this question has been asked, beginning in September 1993, the percent supporting Israel has varied from a low of 37 percent to a high of 48 percent, while the percent supporting the Palestinians has ranged between 10 and 21 percent. At no time has the gap between Israeli support and Palestinian support fallen below 23 percentage points (40 percent and 17 percent support respectively was reported in September 2001).

Still, this question is focused on the somewhat nebulous issue of "sympathy." What about the concrete issue of government policies? Perhaps here Americans would prefer what critics of Israel might consider a more "even-handed" approach.

Actually, they don't. In August 2005, the Pew researchers asked, "thinking about the Mideast situation these days, do you think the U.S. should take Israel's side more, less, or about as much as in the past?" Forty-seven percent of Americans said "as much," and another 16 percent said "more."

But then, a critic might suggest, perhaps the problem is that the Americans surveyed don't understand the gravity of the situation. Do they realize that America's support for Israel is widely unpopular on the global stage? Perhaps if the general public knew this, they might change their minds and reject the Israeli alliance.

Once again—no. The Pew researchers considered this issue as well. Here is what they found:

The American public is not unaware that U.S. policies in the Middle East have strengthened anti-American feelings around the world in recent years. In a November 2005 poll, about four-in-ten (39%) of the U.S. public said that U.S. support for Israel is a major reason that people around the world are unhappy with the U.S. (though far more fingered U.S. wealth and power and the war on terrorism as major reasons). Another 39% saw it as a minor reason.[7]

Given the real prevalence of both anti-Israel and anti-U.S. sentiment around the world, this is a realistic assessment of global public opinion. But note that the Americans surveyed by Pew, while acknowledging these international realities, *still favor* continued support for Israel.

Maybe it's time for the "blame-the-Lobby" gang to admit the truth: the American people actually *like* Israel and want to keep the alliance between our two nations strong. It's not a matter—as Mearsheimer and Walt imply—of a clever minority twisting government policy as an "indifferent" majority looks the other way. Instead, the bulk of Americans have made their preferences clear, and U.S. support for Israel reflects their wishes.

The myth: *The leading Jewish American and Israeli American organizations give slavish support to Israeli policies, no matter whether Israel is right or wrong.*

The reality: *Robust debate about Israeli policies is commonplace not only in Israel but also in the United States, both inside and outside the Jewish* *community. That's as it should be, and Jewish American organizations support and encourage such diversity of opinion.*

In a perverse way, it's flattering that community leaders like myself and the heads of other influential organizations are so often credited with the power to control the words and beliefs of our fellow Jews (to say nothing of the U.S. Congress and State Department). However, it's just not true.

The Jews are a famously individualistic, argumentative, strong-willed people. (Just read God's complaints about us in the Torah if you don't believe me!) They haven't changed their nature in the past 6,000 years, and they won't do it just because a community leader expresses an opinion!

In any case, there have been plenty of instances in which the Anti-Defamation League (ADL) has itself criticized Israeli policy. We're not in the business of setting foreign policy—for Israel, the United States, or any other country; nor are we a political party or international diplomats. But as an organization devoted to tolerance, democracy, and human rights, we criticize governments whenever they take steps that weaken those values and support bigotry, repression, and hatred—and that includes Israel.

In some cases, our criticism is conveyed in private, during personal meetings with Israeli leaders. In other cases, we go public. Of the many examples of the latter that I could cite, I'll mention just a few.

In 1981, Israel effectively annexed the Golan Heights, a plateau on the border between Israel and Syria that had been captured by Israeli forces during the 1967 and 1973 wars. The area had been under Israeli military administration since 1967; the 1981 move was not legally de-clared an "annexation" but simply involved formalizing Israeli control, imposing Israeli civilian rule, and offering the option of Israeli citizen-ship to residents of the area. Although many Israelis, including some military leaders, regard the Golan Heights as essential to the nation's security (and viewed their seizure as a desirable step for the long-term safety of Israel's people), we at ADL condemned this action, believing that it may have created a needless obstacle to peace.

Today, there are some 32 Israeli settlements in the Golan Heights, containing around 17,000 residents. If and when a return of the Golan Heights to Syria is negotiated, these settlements will almost surely need to be dismantled. In addition, a demilitarized zone that will pre-vent either nation from using the Golan Heights as a staging ground for attacks on the other will be important. Unfortunately, negotiating these and other details has proven very difficult—all of which under-scores the fact that Israel's unilateral action in claiming the area in 1981 has proven to be just another stage in the "Golan Heights prob-lem," not a solution to it.

A second example. In 1991, Ariel Sharon was serving as Israel's Minister of Housing and Construction. In that year, he worked with members of the Ateret Cohanim settler group to try to gain control of properties in the Muslim Quarter of the Old City of Jerusalem. He even tried to "fast-track" a settlement plan for a site in the area known as Herod's Gate, earmarked for immigrants from the Soviet Union. It was a terrible idea, one that would have needlessly damaged relation-ships between Arabs and Jews in Jerusalem and possibly impeded the peace process, and ADL spoke out forcefully against it. Fortunately, Sharon's plan was stopped: the town planner of Jerusalem pointed out that it would have violated principles designed to preserve the Old City's historic and cultural value and ruled the plan illegal.

A third example. In 2002, the Israeli parliament passed an amendment to the Citizenship Law that restricted the rights of Palestinians who marry Israeli citizens from living in Israel. It was an ill-conceived bill, written in response to a serious problem—attacks on Israeli civilians by Palestinian suicide bombers. But the "solution" offered by this law was less than relevant. Critics pointed out that, of 100,000 Palestinians who had become Israeli citizens through marriage, only around twenty had been suspected of terrorist-related activities. What's more, the very existence of such a law opens Israel to the accusation of being prejudiced, since the law discriminates between two different classes of citizens based on their ethnic background. All in all, we feel this law damages the principles on which a democracy like Israel should be based.

Despite the ADL's opposition and that of other groups such as Human Rights Watch, the law was renewed each year since its original passage, and in May 2006, it was narrowly upheld (by a six-to-five vote) by the Israeli High Court.

These are just a few examples of times when ADL found itself publicly disagreeing with the Israeli government on a specific issue. In taking these positions, we found ourselves in agreement with some of our fellow Jews, in disagreement with others. We had allies among some members of the Israel Parliament (of various parties), and we experienced opposition from others. All of this is part of the normal give-and-take of democratic debate, which is one of the great strengths of Israel, just as it is of the United States.

Slavish, uniform support for Israeli policies? At ADL, we don't believe in it and we wouldn't think of demanding it from anyone else.

The myth: *Powerful lobbies—including the Israel Lobby—have virtually unchallenged power to dictate public policies to their liking, often to the detriment of the national interest.*

The reality: *Like most lobby groups in the United States, the Jewish American lobby organizations face constant conflict with other groups that generally favor opposing policies. Though journalists and interested parties sometimes like to depict particular lobbying groups as "all-powerful" or "unstoppable," there really is no such thing as a lobby that always gets its way—which is a good thing for America's pluralistic democracy. It's true of the Israel lobby, just as it's true of every other lobby that does business in Washington.*

Just consider some of the groups that are held up as examples of vast power in Washington.

Many call the American Association of Retired Persons (AARP), with its 50 million members and its vast war chest, the most powerful lobby in America. And in recent years we've seen the influence of AARP in its (so-far) successful battle to defend traditional Social Security against attempts to privatize the plan. Does this mean AARP is all-powerful or that it is unopposed? Not at all. While AARP defends public Social Security, the vast and wealthy financial industry, representing Wall Street firms, brokerage houses, commercial banks, and insurance companies, would like to see Social Security privatized, thereby creating millions of private investment accounts for them to manage.

What about the teachers' unions, like the National Education Association? In their battles to defend public schools against funding cuts, voucher systems, and charter schools, they are opposed by taxpayer groups such as the National Taxpayers' Union, conservative and libertarian think tanks and lobby groups, and private companies like the Edison Schools that are looking for the big contracts that privatization could bring.

Then there's the National Rifle Association (NRA), which has won a reputation for enormous clout due to its successful battles against gun control. But the NRA doesn't have the field all to itself. It must battle against groups that favor gun control, including the powerful lobbies on behalf of police and correctional officers, crime victims, and citizens groups.

Each of these powerful lobby groups faces strong countervailing opposition. And the same is true of the much-vaunted Israel lobby.

For example, there is the Arab lobby. There are twenty U.S. diplomats with experience serving in the Arab world for every one with similar experience in Israel. These Arabists within the State Department form a powerful group with an enormous influence on government thinking. There is also a large infrastructure of Arabist think tanks, university chairs, and journalists with an interest in or ties to the many Arab nations, all of whom exercise their influence on behalf of "balance" in U.S. Middle East policy. And let's not forget the Saudi lobby.

Then there is the oil industry, one of America's largest, richest, and most politically powerful businesses. It's no accident that the oil companies have enjoyed enormous tax breaks and other special favors over the decades. The current administration is even headed by not one but two former oil industry executives. With their powerful vested interest in maintaining a steady flow of oil from the major Middle Eastern states—including Iraq, Iran, Saudi Arabia, and the emirates of the Persian Gulf—these companies are eager to keep the United States on friendly terms with the Arab nations, and they use their influence to push hard against too strong a U.S. "tilt" toward Israel.

Finally, there are the arms manufacturers, makers of aircraft, and high-tech companies, many of which make billions by selling their wares to the Arab nations. These companies, too, have a strong vested interest in maintaining good relations between the United States and the Arab world—which means minimizing the influence of Israel.

For example, in the one-year period from September 2005 to September 2006, U.S. arms makers booked $21 billion in foreign weapons sales, almost *double* the amount sold in the previous year. Among the major purchasers: Saudi Arabia ($5.8 billion worth of Black Hawk helicopters, Abrams and Bradley armored land vehicles, and other gear); Bahrain, Jordan, and the United Arab Emirates ($1 billion for more Black Hawk helicopters); Oman (a $48 million antitank missile system), and several other Arab and Muslim nations.[8]

Suppose a new, strongly pro-Israel administration were to promulgate a new policy sharply curtailing arms sales to Arab countries that potentially threaten Israel. Do you imagine that the U.S. companies that profit from these and other lucrative weapons contracts would roll over quietly? Not very likely.

Yes, it's true that the pro-Israel lobby is a powerful one on Capitol Hill and in the White House. Does it face no strong opposition? That'll be the day!

The myth: *ADL and other "Jewish lobby" groups push a hard-line, hawkish political point of view that doesn't represent the mainstream of Jewish opinion in either Israel or the United States.*

The reality: *As an organization dedicated to the freedom of Jews, the right of Israel to exist as a Jewish homeland, and the protection of civil rights for all people, ADL has inevitably gotten involved in some politically controversial topics. One of the challenges we face on a regular basis is figuring out exactly how to position ourselves so as to serve our core mission without becoming embroiled in irrelevant or distracting battles. Making these choices isn't always easy, and we've made an occasional misstep. But our overall objective is clear, and as long as we pursue it single-mindedly, we don't get into trouble.*

It's simply inaccurate to say that the ADL, or indeed, most other Jewish organizations, is a "hawkish," "hard line," or right-wing organization. Throughout the history of modern Israel, since its founding in 1948, over nearly seven decades, the government has shifted control repeatedly between very liberal and very conservative parties (as is true in the United States and many other democracies). Throughout this time, the ADL has supported *every* Israeli government—right, left, or center. Why wouldn't we? We're an organization devoted to the rights and freedoms of *every* Jew, and for that matter of every human being—not just the rights of people who support a particular party or political persuasion. And since we believe that the survival and success of Israel as a nation is crucial to the long-term health and freedom of the Jewish people, we support Israeli governments of every stripe. They all want what's best for the people of Israel, and so do we.

Do individual supporters of ADL—including our elected leaders—have personal positions on political issues? Naturally. Do we hold opinions—sometimes strong ones—about such controversial matters as the formation of a Palestinian state, Israeli-Arab relations, control of the territories, and the kinds of antiterror tactics Israel should use to defend itself? Of course. But ADL doesn't take positions on these issues as an organization, nor do we establish or defend any "party line" on these matters. Within our offices—and within our own families—there are fierce disagreements about them and often heated debates. All of that is fine—and it certainly never prevents us from coming together and working jointly on behalf of those causes that are at the heart of ADL's mission.

So the idea that the "Jewish lobby" pushes a monolithic, hawkish point of view on Israeli policies is simply false, at least as far as ADL is concerned. What about other influential Jewish American organizations, such as the American Israel Public Affairs Committee (AIPAC) and the American Jewish Committee (AJC)? Is the myth accurate in reference to them?

It's true that there has been some rightward drift among some Jewish American leaders in recent years. Perhaps this was inevitable. A generation ago, Jewish Americans were among the most liberal, and the most reliably Democratic voters, of any ethnic, religious, racial, or demographic group in the country. The idea that this would continue forever was probably always unrealistic (as much as Democratic party leaders would probably have liked it to continue). As the entire country has slowly shifted toward the conservative end of the spectrum, American Jews have shifted with them. They are still relatively liberal-leaning and relatively Democratic in their voting. What was generally once a 90/10 split between Democrats and Republicans among Jews has now become something like a 75/25 split—still, not a source of comfort among Republican leaders.

So, yes, Jews in America have become a little more conservative than they once were—not only on foreign policy issues but also on economics, race, the environment, education, health care, and many other topics. However, they are very far from representing a mono-lithic conservative bloc. In fact, it would be more accurate to say that the rightward shift of American Jews since 1980 has made the commu-nity, if anything, *less* monolithic than it once was—less monolithically liberal and Democratic, that is.

As for AIPAC, the AJC, and other Jewish organizations: I can't speak for the leaders of those groups, who are very articulate and quite capable of defending themselves. However, I would make one observation about the *nature* of these groups that many critics ignore. The purpose of an organized group, when doing advocacy through lobbying, is to encourage the passage of legislation and the establishment of administration policies that favor the interests that the lobbyists endorse. The only way a lobbyist can achieve this is by having positive connections with the people who are in government—members of Congress, administration officials, staffers at the various agencies and departments, and so on. It is all well and good to talk about the power exerted by public pressure or financial donations, but these don't have a lot of influence unless they are accompanied by strong personal relationships. If a lobbyist can't sit down at the same table with people in government and *talk* with them about matters of concern, very little will get done—no matter how many checks the lobbyist may write or press releases he may issue.

The inevitable consequence of this is that, as the party makeup and political ideology of government personnel changes, so do the leanings of lobbyists. In eras like the 1940s and the 1960s, when all three branches of the federal government were dominated by liberal Democrats, the most effective lobby groups in Washington were largely staffed by liberal Democrats. Naturally so—people like that had the best chance of influencing government simply because they could sit down with their counterparts and "talk the same language." Of course, there were conservatives and Republicans represented in the lobbying community—no significant political group in America is ever truly monolithic—but liberal Democrats dominated.

Since 1980, Washington has changed. For 19 of the 27 years since then, Republicans have controlled the White House, and between 1994 and 2006, Republicans controlled Congress as well. Inevitably, the lobbying community has shifted toward the conservative and Republican end of the spectrum. This only makes sense. If you (as a lobbying group) need to deal with, negotiate with, and work with a power structure that is dominated by Republicans, you probably want to have at least a few Republicans around to help you! The makeup of groups like AIPAC, ADL, and AJC have evolved, in large part, in response to this reality.

So, yes, the leadership of Jewish community groups has moved somewhat toward the right—not because of some kind of conspiracy or power grab, but as part of the overall evolution of the country and shifting political winds in Washington. If and when the tide turns back toward liberalism and the Democratic party—a change that many observers think is inevitable and that may have already begun—you can probably expect advocacy organizations, including those representing the Jewish community, to follow suit. It's in the nature of what we do.

The myth: *The Israel Lobby enforces—or seeks to enforce—ideological conformity on U.S. college campuses.*

The reality: *As college professors themselves, Mearsheimer and Walt are naturally concerned about academic freedom, and it would greatly strengthen their argument about the power of the Israel Lobby to control* *debate in the United States if they could show that its tentacles extend to America's college campuses.*

Unfortunately for the authors, the idea that colleges and universities in the United States are dominated by pro-Israeli voices is absurdly laughable, even more so than their claims that the Lobby controls Congress, the State Department, and the White House. Thus, Mearsheimer and Walt are forced to do a lot of hedging and filling in their discussion of the Lobby and academia. They admit that "The Lobby has had the most difficulty stifling debate about Israel on college campuses," and in mild desperation they list many instances in which pro-Israel advocates merely criticized or disagreed with specific faculty members or university programs. For example, the fact that writings by the late Palestinian scholar Edward Said provoked "hundreds of e-mails, letters, and journalistic accounts that call on [Columbia University] to denounce Said and to either sanction or fire him" is cited as evidence of the power of the Lobby on campus. The fact that Said never *was* denounced, sanctioned, or fired is apparently irrelevant.[9]

The truth is that American college campuses are enormously diverse from almost every point of view—and that includes ideologically. In fact, many campuses have become hotbeds of anti-Zionist, pro-Palestinian, and, in a few cases, outright anti-Semitic activism. Jewish organizations are working hard to try to hold their own, but their voices are often being drowned out by those of militant anti-Israel groups.

Many of these groups are members of the umbrella group known as the Palestine Solidarity Movement (PSM), which is leading a nationwide campaign to portray the Palestinian cause as a struggle for justice against the "racist and apartheid" State of Israel and to encourage colleges to withdraw their investment funds from Israel—the so-called divestment movement. Dozens of professors and hundreds of students have signed petitions in support of this movement, although no major university has yet agreed to its demands. The PSM has refused to condemn terrorism against Israelis, stating that "as a solidarity movement, it is not our place to dictate the strategies or tactics adopted by the Palestinian people in their struggle for liberation." It has held major student conferences at Berkeley, the University of Michigan, Rutgers University, and Ohio State University.[10]

Of course, advocates of the Palestinian cause are free to promulgate their ideas on college campuses as elsewhere in democratic societies. And they are doing so with a great deal of energy and quite a bit of success. Once again, reality gives the lie to the Mearsheimer and Walt contention that "alternative views" are nowhere to be found.

As often happens, the testimony of the "anti-Lobby" critics actually serves to undermine their own claims. Here is a paragraph from an essay by Tony Judt, a noted European historian and a professor at New York University, who has weighed in prominently in defense of Mearsheimer and Walt (and became the center of a heated controversy I'll detail in the next chapter):

Here at New York University I was teaching this past month a class on post-war Europe. I was trying to explain to young

Americans the importance of the Spanish Civil War in the political memory of Europeans and why Franco's Spain has such
a special place in our moral imagination: as a reminder of
lost struggles, a symbol of oppression in an age of liberalism
and freedom, and a land of shame that people boycotted for
its crimes and repression. I cannot think, I told the students,
of any country that occupies such a pejorative space in democratic public consciousness today. You are wrong, one
young woman replied: What about Israel? To my great surprise most of the class—including many of the sizable Jewish contingent—nodded approval. The times they are
indeed a-changing.[11]

It's an interesting anecdote. And while it is dangerous to draw general conclusions on the basis of any one anecdote (although Judt himself describes this as "One example among many"), it is hard to
reconcile this story—set, mind you, on a liberal college campus in the
heart of a city with a large and vibrant Jewish community—with the
image of an academic world where pro-Israeli orthodoxy is running
rampant. If the Israel Lobby has mounted such a powerful propaganda
effort to indoctrinate college students, where did Tony Judt's students
acquire the (frankly absurd) notion that Israel is a quasi-fascist regime
comparable to Franco's Spain?

One would think that a scholar like Judt would recognize the dis-
connect between his mythical America where anti-Israeli ideas are
forcibly suppressed and the real America where such views are widely
promulgated. But he doesn't—not even when he describes the discon-
nect himself.

The myth: *Jews have used their political power in the United States to ensure that Israeli interests inevitably prevail in the shaping of American foreign policy.*

The reality: *It's true that the United States and Israel have a strong alliance. I'm happy to be able to say this because I believe such an alliance is in the best interests of both countries as well as in the interests of peace in the Middle East and around the world. But the notion that Israeli interests somehow control U.S. foreign policy is absurd. American governments are no more subservient to the wishes of Israel than they are to the demands of Great Britain, France, Mexico, Japan, or any other important U.S. ally.*

History shows that there have been many times when the U.S. government followed a foreign policy agenda that differed from the one that either the Israeli government or American Jewish supporters of Israel favored. Again, I'll offer just a few examples to demonstrate the point.

In 1981, the newly installed Reagan administration announced plans to sell five U.S.-made E–3 Airborne Warning and Control System aircraft (colloquially known as AWACs) to the government of Saudi Arabia. These were among the most advanced military equipment then in existence, equipped with a powerful antenna capable of detecting and tracking other aircraft within an area of 175,000 square miles.

The government of Israel was very worried about the impact this sale could have on the security of their country and on the prospects for peace in the region, and they made their concerns felt in no uncertain terms. Prime Minister Menachem Begin expressed "profound regret and unreserved opposition" to the proposed sale. And many observers with no particular ax to grind shared Begin's concerns. Senator Edward Kennedy (D-Massachusetts) called it "one of the worst and most dangerous arms sales ever," and his colleague Bob Packwood (R-Oregon) warned that the sale would "promote continued instability in the Middle East."

What happened? Did the power of the Lobby halt the sale? Not at all: after a season of intense lobbying by the Reagan administration, Congress approved the sale in October 1981.

My second example dates from 1991. It was a critical time in the history of the Middle East. The United States had just led an international coalition that had driven the armies of Saddam Hussein from Kuwait in the first Gulf war. A major effort to restart the peace process was being promoted by President George H. W. Bush and his secretary of state, James Baker, with plans being developed for a regional conference to take place in Madrid by the end of the year. Meanwhile, a massive influx of Jews from the Soviet Union was putting economic pressure on Israel and exacerbating tensions with the Palestinians, who feared that the new immigrants might take over portions of the disputed territories.

In this heightened atmosphere, President Bush decided that the time was right to challenge Israel on its policies in the occupied territories. As his vehicle for this challenge, he chose a $10 billion set of loan guarantees that Israeli Prime Minister Yitzhak Shamir had requested. In a combative press conference on September 12, Bush announced that he would recommend that Congress turn down the request. He also complained about the efforts of pro-Israeli spokespeople to change his mind, contrasting the work of "a thousand lobbyists" with his own, supposedly lonely stance on the opposite side: "one little guy down here doing it."[12]

It was a slightly weird performance by the president, one that led to strained relations between the United States and Israel for months to come. But the point is that the president got his way. Congress followed his lead in delaying consideration of the loan guarantees. Israel, for its part, succumbed to U.S. pressure and agreed to participate in the Madrid peace talks. Partly as a result of the tension between the two countries, Shamir was defeated in his effort to win reelection the following June.

Bush had shown that, like any other lobby, the Israel lobby has just as much power as American politicians are willing to grant it—in this case, not very much.

Finally, an example from our own day—one that flies directly in the teeth of the Mearsheimer and Walt thesis.

As I have said, "The Israel Lobby" blames the government of Israel and its U.S. supporters for the American invasion of Iraq in 2003. And it is certainly true that most Israeli leaders regarded Saddam Hussein's regime as a threat to the peace and stability of the Middle East. (So did most leaders throughout the world—but for the moment, we'll let that pass.) But as even Mearsheimer and Walt acknowledge, the government of Israel actually did not rank Iraq as the number one threat to their country in the region. Here is what Mearsheimer and Walt have to say:

> Israelis tend to describe every threat in the starkest terms, but Iran is widely seen as their most dangerous enemy because it is the most likely adversary to acquire nuclear weapons. Virtually all Israelis regard an Islamic country in the Middle East with nuclear weapons as an existential threat. As Israeli defense Minister Binyamin Ben-Eliezer remarked one month before the Iraq war: "Iraq is a problem. . . . But you should understand, if you ask me, today Iran is more dangerous than Iraq."[13]

And the authors go on to quote a number of other prominent Israelis who stated in the run-up to the Iraq war that Iran was a more serious threat to Israel than Iraq.

It's all very alarming, and certainly testifies to the desire of Israeli leaders to influence the thinking of the United States. But Mearsheimer and Walt seem to ignore one salient fact: *The United States chose to attack Iraq, not Iran.* Given the fact that Israel regarded Iran as the primary threat, how does the U.S. decision to invade Iraq instead square with the notion of Israeli "control" of U.S. foreign policy?

As you can understand, those who find the Mearsheimer and Walt thesis dubious have raised this objection in public forums and debates where one of the authors has appeared. The authors' usual response has been something along the lines of, "Well, Israel is worried about *both* countries, and it was always understood that Iraq and Iran would be taken out in sequence." This doesn't explain why the supposedly compliant American policymakers chose to ignore Israel's emphasis on Iran as the primary threat—unless we assume what Mearsheimer and Walt assure us is impossible, that U.S. leaders actually consult U.S. interests rather than Israeli interests when making such decisions.

I should note that, in their essay, Mearsheimer and Walt also named Syria as a likely target of the Lobby.[14] I guess the "sequence" of wars that the authors foretell is really a three-country sequence. But then, it would probably be possible to dig up a statement by some Israeli official musing about the *potential* threat posed by *any* Arab country in the Middle East. That is one of the things responsible government officials do— think about potential threats. Perhaps Mearsheimer and Walt are simply positioning themselves to claim that *any* aggressive action by the United States in the Middle East is driven by Israeli goals.

This is an illustration of one of the convenient qualities of myths: their almost infinite malleability. If you want to believe the worst about Israel and the Jews, you can probably find facts to bolster your arguments. But it's even easier to simply subscribe to a series of fantasies, such as those that Mearsheimer and Walt promulgate. Because they are scarcely tethered to reality, they can be maintained indefinitely no matter what happens in the world, precluding the necessity for the hard, sometimes painful work of *actually thinking* about what is going on and making informed judgments about it.

It certainly explains why myths—including hoary anti-Semitic ones—will always have their appeal to a certain part of the population . . . and why the rest of us must constantly be on the lookout for them.

4

THE POWER OF MISINFORMATION: THE JUDT AFFAIR

I N THE CURRENT CLIMATE OF GLOBAL INSECURITY, CROSS-cultural tension, heightened ideological partisanship, and general anxiety, it was perhaps only a matter of time before the widespread belief that "the Jewish lobby" exercises a stranglehold over foreign policy debate in the United States became attached to one or more specific events—anecdotes that supporters of the most pernicious myths about Jews could point to as "proof" of their allegations.

In the anti-Semitic France of the 1890s, the convenient event onto which the bigots and haters latched was the Dreyfus affair. In Germany between the wars, it was the loss of World War I, which the Hitlerites somehow contrived to blame on Jewish traitors in their midst. In Mc-Carthy-era America, it was the Julius and Ethel Rosenberg spy case. Now, in the early years of the twenty-first century, the new bigots have yet to discover or invent a major "scandal" that they can use as a club for beating up the Jews. But they seem to have seized on a couple of minor ones that may serve as dry runs for a bigger attack that I fear is coming.

Perhaps the most notorious such event is what has become known as the Judt affair. Because I was, unwillingly, a major participant in this event—some would say its villain!—I have some inside knowledge as to what *really* happened. Sadly but unsurprisingly, the facts bear little resemblance to the version that was current at the height of the controversy. And it seems that many people to this day assume that the false accounts widely disseminated in the media are correct.

The purpose of this chapter is to set the record straight—and, more important, to shed light on the realities about American Jews, Israel, foreign policy, and free speech in the United States.

To begin with, who is Tony Judt and why should anyone care about him?

Judt is a well-known European historian, a professor at New York University, and director of its Erich Maria Remarque Institute. He is the author of several books, the most famous of which is perhaps *Postwar: A History of Europe Since 1945,* a runner-up for the 2006 Pulitzer Prize for General Non-Fiction.[1]

Judt has also been a lightning rod for controversy. A Jew who was raised in London by parents of Eastern European descent, Judt lived in Israel for a period of time and served in its military, working as a driver and translator for the Israel Defense Forces just after the 1967 Six-Day War. Nonetheless, in recent decades he has become a harsh critic of the very idea of a Jewish state.

In a widely discussed 2003 article titled "Israel: The Alternative," Judt wrote:

> In a world where nations and peoples increasingly intermingle and intermarry at will; where cultural and national impediments to communication have all but collapsed; where more and more of us have multiple elective identities and would feel falsely constrained if we had to answer to just one of them; in such a world Israel is truly an anachronism. And not just an anachronism but a dysfunctional one. In today's "clash of cultures" between open, pluralist democracies and belligerently intolerant, faith-driven ethno-states, Israel actually risks falling into the wrong camp.

"Israel," he concluded, "is bad for the Jews."[2]

Perhaps Judt wishes he could turn back the clock and undo the series of events that led to the birth of Israel as a Jewish state in 1948. But obviously that is impossible. Israel exists today as a flourishing nation of over six million people, a powerful economic and military force, an influential player on the world stage. Israel is not going anywhere. But it remains embattled and, in the eyes of many people—

including Tony Judt—it is somehow "controversial," its very existence an embarrassment, a problem to be solved.

What is Judt's solution? That Israel should become a "binational" state in which Jews and Arabs should have equal status and power in government, even if this should lead, in time, to a country dominated by Arabs. And indeed, demographic statistics suggest that this is exactly what would happen. As of 2006, the population growth rate within Israel was estimated at 1.18 percent annually; in the West Bank, at 3.06 percent. With the 2.4 million Arabs in the territories already representing some forty percent of the combined populations of Israel and the West Bank, a unified binational state could have a majority Arab population within a generation.[3]

Judt's article was an honest attempt to grapple with some serious problems confronting Israel. These include the difficulty of balancing the country's role as a haven and homeland for a religious and ethnic group with the democratic imperative and the equality that implies, as well as the demographic pressure exerted on Israel by the greater rate of population growth among the nation's Arabs as compared with its Jews. But these demographic realities are themselves a powerful reason why the great majority of Israel's citizens will never accept the binational solution. Judt himself admitted that his proposal for a binational state was probably impractical and defended it on the ground that, "In any case, no one I know of has a better idea." He added:

A binational state in the Middle East would require the emergence, among Jews and Arabs alike, of a new political class.

The very idea is an unpromising mix of realism and utopia, hardly an auspicious place to begin. But the alternatives are far, far worse.[4]

Let me be clear: I strongly disagree with Judt's position, although of course I respect his right to advocate it as a matter of free speech. I think his position is based on some fundamental misreadings of history and human character. Judt writes:

For many years, Israel had a special meaning for the Jewish people. After 1948 it took in hundreds of thousands of helpless survivors who had nowhere else to go; without Israel their condition would have been desperate in the extreme. Israel needed Jews, and Jews needed Israel.[5]

What Judt says here about the meaning of Israel for the Jews is perfectly correct. Where he is wrong, I think, is in his use of the past tense. Israel *still has* a special meaning for the Jewish people. It is still our ultimate refuge in time of need, the one country on Earth where we *know* there will never be anything for us to fear from the powers that be, the one nation that will take us in even if the whole world should somehow turn against us. Jews still need Israel, and I for one—along with millions of other Jews—am not ready to abandon her.

In any case, one thing should be clear: Tony Judt's position is that of a man who fundamentally disapproves of the existence of Israel as a Jewish state. As far as I know, Judt has not explicitly demanded that Israel be destroyed. But given realities on the ground—especially the unmistakable demographic trends—Judt's call for a binational state is simply a proposal for slow-motion suicide. A binational Israel will inevitably become a majority-Arab Palestine. In the words of Leon Wieseltier, "I have never met anybody of any persuasion who believes that Judt's call for a one-state solution to the Israeli-Palestinian conflict in 'Israel: The Alternative' was not a call for the abolition of the Jewish state."[6] You can't understand the feelings of pro-Israel Jews toward Tony Judt without recognizing this fact.

Try to imagine how the average American might feel about someone who advocates the overthrow and dissolution of the United States government, and the absorption, if such a thing were possible, of the United States into some neighboring country, and you'll have some inkling of the strong feelings that Tony Judt inspires.

Obviously, Tony Judt's prescription for solving the problems of the Middle East has not found favor with the vast majority of Israelis. It has also been rejected by most Americans, both at the grass-roots level and among scholars, experts, academics, authors, and policy leaders. As I've noted, approval of the existence of Israel as a Jewish state and support for the idea that the United States (and its democratic allies) should stand with Israel in its efforts to defend itself against assaults from hostile neighbors remains extremely high in almost every American opinion poll. No wonder most politicians take the same position. It doesn't take much genius to endorse a policy that the great majority of experts favor and that also happens to be extremely popular among the voters.

Under the circumstances, Tony Judt, a historian with aspirations to shape international politics, can't be happy to find himself stuck among a small minority of people who share his views and have relatively little influence in the places that matter—the halls of Congress, the State Department, the Oval Office, and, above all, the voting booths. It is perhaps natural that he should feel like "a voice crying in the wilderness," a wise pundit whose wisdom is somehow, inexplicably being ignored by the very people who should, in his view, be embracing it.

Such a feeling is fertile ground for the growth of conspiracy theories.

It's not surprising, then, that Tony Judt is among the American scholars and pundits who feel strong sympathy with the Mearsheimer and Walt thesis. If it's true that a powerful cabal of Jews controls U.S. foreign policy for their own benefit and actively works to silence dissent, then this would provide a convenient and face-saving explanation for why Judt's recommendations for fixing the Middle East have fallen on deaf ears. "It's not that there's anything wrong with my ideas," Judt can claim, "It's the sinister influence of that darned Lobby!"

(An aside: Isn't it likely that some such feeling underlies much of the emotional appeal that a belief in Jewish conspiracies seems to hold for so many people, even if not for an academic such as Tony Judt? It's comforting to imagine that one's lack of success—in the marketplace, in academia, in politics—can be blamed on some evil force bent on thwarting the good and the deserving. Thus, in a funny way, belief in a

Jewish cabal may actually be a mark of personal vanity. And the more powerful the cabal, the better! As poet Robert Frost once wisely observed, "It is immodest of a man to think of himself as going down before the worst forces ever mobilized by God."[7] I think many of the conspiracymongers are guilty of this sort of immodesty.)

It's also not surprising that Tony Judt's voice was one of the earliest to be raised in support of Mearsheimer and Walt.

In April 2006, Judt penned an op-ed column in the *New York Times* titled "A Lobby, Not a Conspiracy," in which he described the Mearsheimer and Walt paper, summarized their thesis, and defended them from the criticism that their work had already begun to attract.[8]

The nature of Judt's defense was somewhat curious. Although he acknowledged that "Critics have charged that their scholarship is shoddy," he made no effort to defend their scholarship. (As we've seen in our own analysis of "The Israel Lobby," that would be quite difficult to do.) Instead, he tut-tutted about the *tone* of the criticism while ignoring its substance: "This somewhat hysterical response," he wrote, "is regrettable."

Judt went on to finesse the actual issues that Mearsheimer and Walt raised. He asked, "Does the Israel Lobby affect our foreign policy choices? Of course—that is one of its goals." And, of course this is noncontroversial since *by definition* any lobbying effort is intended to have an "effect" on government policies. The difference between "domination" or "control" and "effect" is the crucial one, which Judt obscured.

He then asked, "But does pressure to support Israel distort American decisions? That's a matter of judgment." And on this crucial question, Judt hedged, admitting that, for example, American support for Israel was probably *not* a crucial factor in the decision to invade Iraq.

So having ignored the major criticism of Mearsheimer and Walt's paper (that their scholarship was shoddy), finessed the issues raised by one of their two chief theories (that the Israel Lobby dominates U.S. Middle Eastern policy), and cast doubt on the other (that the same Lobby has driven foreign policy choices harmful to America), Judt retreated to a fall-back position—that the failure of the mainstream media to thoroughly publicize and debate the Mearsheimer and Walt thesis was *in itself* a demonstration of the correctness of their position!

As Judt put it:

The essay and the issues it raises for American foreign policy have been prominently dissected and discussed overseas. In America, however, it's been another story: virtual silence in the mainstream media. Why? There are several plausible explanations. One is that a relatively obscure academic paper is of little concern to general-interest readers. Another is that claims about disproportionate Jewish public influence are hardly original—and debate over them inevitably attracts interest from the political extremes. And then there is the view that Washington is anyway awash in "lobbies" of this sort, pressuring policymakers and distorting their choices.

Each of these considerations might reasonably account for the mainstream press's initial indifference to the Mearsheimer-Walt essay. But they don't convincingly explain the continued silence even after the article aroused stormy debate in the academy, within the Jewish community, among the opinion magazines and Web sites, and in the rest of the world. I think there is another element in play: fear. Fear of being thought to legitimize talk of a "Jewish conspiracy"; fear of being thought anti-Israel; and thus, in the end, fear of licensing the expression of anti-Semitism.[9]

In other words, Mearsheimer and Walt may have been accused of being poor scholars, sloppy thinkers, and wrong on the facts—but the "fact" that the mainstream press has disregarded their essay proves they are right after all!

One might think that shoddy scholarship and a dubious central thesis would be enough to render "The Israel Lobby" of limited interest to the mainstream media. The additional factors Judt himself cites—the fact that the essay was in fact "a relatively obscure academic paper" of the kind that the general public almost always ignores, and the fact that the main theme of the paper was "hardly original"— would seem to make it perfectly obvious why Mearsheimer and Walt weren't being treated as front-page news in most media outlets.

But no. Apparently, according to Tony Judt, any essay claiming that Jews control the public discourse *must* be widely promoted, discussed, analyzed, and debated—or else the very thesis it promotes is thereby definitively proven! (When I was growing up in Brooklyn, we used to call this a "heads I win, tails you lose" proposition.)

As I say, this seemed a curious way to defend Mearsheimer and Walt. But Judt's argument carried enough weight with the editors of the *New York Times* for them to turn over a large chunk of their prestigious op-ed real estate to his 1,289-word essay. (This in itself would seem to belie the notion that the mainstream media refuse to discuss the issue of Israeli influence. But, again, ordinary standards of logic apparently don't apply when the subject is Israel and the Jews.)

One last point on this essay. Judt's op-ed was published on April 19, 2006. That is less than four weeks after Mearsheimer's and Walt's essay was originally published in the *London Review of Books*. It's a little strange that Judt should believe that a lapse of four weeks between the publication of "a relatively obscure academic paper" and its dissection in the mainstream media suggests that debate is being stifled. When academic ideas filter into the mainstream—which they rarely do—it almost always takes time, generally measured in months or years, not weeks.

Here is a comparison. When Samuel P. Huntington published his now-famous essay, "The Clash of Civilizations," in *Foreign Affairs* magazine in the summer of 1993, he simultaneously submitted a much shorter version of his thesis to the *New York Times*, which appeared on June 6 of that year. Did either article spark an immediate flood of responses and debate in the mainstream media? Not at all. In fact, other than a single letter to the editor responding to the op-ed column, the *New York Times* itself didn't publish any commentary on Huntington's thesis until August 28, when the "clash of civilizations" concept was mentioned in a column by Owen Harries.

Thus, it took almost three months for any writer in the single most influential outlet of the mainstream media to mention and

respond to Huntington's controversial essay. That's how long it nor-
mally takes for complex ideas related to specialized and controversial
topics to be absorbed, evaluated, and discussed. Yet, Tony Judt considered it outrageous that his endorsement of Mearsheimer and Walt was
the first article to "break the silence" in the *New York Times*—just four
weeks after the original essay was published. At best, this was disingenuous on Judt's part. But regardless of his motives, it was another example of the kind of double standard that critics of Israel and the Jews
often seem to get away with.

Judt's defense of Mearsheimer and Walt continued in other ven-
ues. In May 2006, he published a lengthy article in Israel's *Ha'aretz*
newspaper that decried the country's loss of the moral high ground
due to its "occupation and repression" of the Palestinian territories
and the consequent loss of international respect and sympathy for Israel. It is time, he declared, for Israel to "grow up" as a nation by acknowledging and renouncing its sins. And the Mearsheimer-Walt
article, he said, would play a positive role in this transformation by
forcing a reevaluation of the U.S. role as an uncritical supporter of Israel. However, Judt's specific policy prescriptions for the new, "ma-
ture" Israel were rather sketchy:

> Precisely because the country [Israel] is an object of such uni-
> versal mistrust and resentment—because people expect so lit-
> tle from Israel today—a truly statesmanlike shift in its policies
> (dismantling of major settlements, opening unconditional
> negotiations with Palestinians, calling Hamas' bluff by offer-
> ing the movement's leaders something serious in return for

recognition of Israel and a cease-fire) could have dispropor-
tionately beneficial effects.[10]

As people who live face to face with mortal enemies have reason to
know, the devil is in the details. What is the "something serious" the Israelis could offer Hamas that would satisfy the leaders of that terror-
sponsoring organization and persuade them to allow Israel to live in
peace? As we've seen, Judt is already on record as favoring a binational
solution that, over time, is virtually certain to transform Israel into an
Arab-dominated state. Is that his "something serious"? If so, what exactly is so "statesmanlike" about a national offer to self-destruct?

Judt's next effort to proselytize on behalf of Mearsheimer and
Walt proved to be something of a prelude to the Judt affair proper. On
September 28, 2006, a standing-room-only crowd at New York's his-
toric Cooper Union hall witnessed a debate sponsored by the *London
Review of Books* on the question, "The Israel Lobby—Does It Have Too
Much Influence on U.S. Foreign Policy?" Judt was teamed with Rashid
Khalidi of Columbia University and John Mearsheimer himself to
argue for the affirmative; arguing on the opposite side of the issue
were Martin Indyk, Dennis Ross, and former Israeli cabinet minister
Shlomo Ben-Ami. The moderator was Anne-Marie Slaughter, dean of
the Woodrow Wilson School at Princeton University.

By all accounts, the debate was a spirited one, with supporters on
both sides audibly cheering sallies by their champions and, when the
dust had settled, claiming overall victory for the evening. Were many
hearts and minds changed by the charges the debaters exchanged or

the accusations they leveled? It's doubtful. Press reports and comments from those in attendance mostly reflected the apparent prior leanings of the respondents. Of course, the very *existence* of the debate and the widespread publicity it received suggests the hollowness of Mearsheimer and Walt's claim that those who challenge the "orthodox" position vis-à-vis Israel are routinely blocked from appearing in public forums.

In any case, this series of events—Judt's *New York Times* op-ed column, his article in *Ha'aretz,* and his participation in the *London Review* debate—made it clear that Judt had seized the Mearsheimer and Walt thesis and embraced it as his own.

Shortly thereafter, we at the Anti-Defamation League (ADL) starting getting calls from people asking about rumors they'd heard about follow-up activities by Tony Judt. Was it true that the Polish consulate would be sponsoring a speech by Tony Judt denouncing the power of the "Jewish lobby"? We got two or three such calls.

When we hear rumors about potentially bigoted, biased, or anti-Semitic speech, we feel obliged to try to track them down. It's one of the legitimate roles played by the Anti-Defamation League on behalf of America's Jewish community. When the rumors turn out to be true, we take action—most often by publicly criticizing the bigoted statements or behaviors, occasionally by calling for more forceful condemnation or actions. When the rumors turn out to be false, we communicate the truth as widely as we can. False accusations of bigotry serve no one. Those who have done nothing wrong deserve to be defended, and we've played that role many times.

When we were asked about Tony Judt, we investigated. We discovered that Judt was indeed scheduled to speak at the Polish consulate on October 3, 2006. His lecture, titled "The Israel Lobby & U.S. Foreign Policy," would be under the auspices of a group called Network 20/20, which describes itself as "an independent membership organization that helps prepare next generation leaders in the U.S. to participate meaningfully in public diplomacy and in the creation and execution of policies promoting global public security."[11]

The fact that Tony Judt would be giving a speech was, in itself, far from scandalous. His freedom of speech, guaranteed by the First Amendment, is as important and precious to us at ADL as it is to Tony Judt himself, and we would always defend it. But when a person takes an anti-Israel position that we regard as far out of the mainstream, we feel it's important to understand his message, track its dissemination, and, wherever possible, ensure that it receives a fair and honest response. We can't stop biased speech, but we can work hard to ensure that the truth is also heard.

The first step was to get the facts straight. (Rumors and distortions quickly gather around emotional issues like this one, and separating them from reality is important and often difficult.) In an effort to do this our director of European Affairs called the Polish consulate twice. He left messages with officials he knew there and received no call back.

Meanwhile, the date of the supposed appearance by Tony Judt was drawing near. On the very day that the speech was scheduled, our director of European Affairs called the consulate one last time. In an effort to get the attention of the Polish officials, he left a message saying,

"Abe Foxman, national director of the Anti-Defamation League, is try-ing to make contact. Please call him back." He then left his own phone number at the end of the message.

Maybe the sense of urgency in his voice got through, because this time the vice consul, a man named Krzysztopf Kasprzyk, phoned him back within a half hour—some four hours prior to the scheduled talk. "No, the Polish Consulate is not *sponsoring* any speech by Tony Judt," he explained. "We have simply rented space in our offices to this group called Network 20/20. They are responsible for organizing the speech and for its content. Can you tell me why ADL is concerned?"

My colleague responded, "If you knew anything about Tony Judt, you would understand. I suggest you try looking him up on Google." And there the conversation ended.

He called the people who had contacted ADL about the rumor and reported exactly what had happened. As far as we knew, at this point the speech by Tony Judt at the Polish consulate was still on track.

Two hours later, my associate got another call. It was about one and a half hours before Tony Judt was scheduled to speak, and Kasprzyk was on the line. "I just wanted to let you know," the vice consul said, "that we've decided to cancel the Tony Judt speech. He will not be appearing at the Polish consulate, under our auspices or anyone else's."

I remember vividly my immediate response when my colleague poked his head into my office and reported this surprising new development. "That's a very dumb thing for them to do." And I remember exactly why I said it. The vice consul meant well. Perhaps he'd googled the name of Tony Judt—and perhaps he'd been concerned or even appalled by what he'd read. But to cancel the speech, especially at the last possible minute, was a foolish step to take. It smacked of censorship and suppression of speech, since it meant that Network 20/20 would not have time to find a new venue or to reschedule Tony Judt's appearance. It also created the appearance that the Polish consulate was responding to "pressure" from Jews and from Jewish organizations like ADL—courting controversy that would be unnecessary, divisive, and distracting.

And of course, that's exactly what happened.

What do I think the Polish consulate should have done instead?

In the first place, it would be wise for someone in their offices to routinely check the backgrounds and credentials of organizations and individuals who want to use their premises for public meetings, speeches, or appearances. Never mind Tony Judt—if you allow groups to rent space without knowing whom you're dealing with, you will eventually find yourself hosting talks by people who will *really* embarrass you, whether they are neo-Nazis, white supremacists, advocates of violence, extreme religious fanatics, or (yes) avowed anti-Semites. I found it stunning that this was apparently not the case at the Polish consulate.

If this had been done, the Polish consulate could have made an informed, thoughtful decision as to whether or not Tony Judt is someone they want to appear to be supporting in a public forum. Maybe they would have opted to host the presentation after all, which would have been their right. They might have issued a press release or some other public message in which they stated, in effect, "We don't necessarily agree with any of Tony Judt's political positions, but we support his freedom of speech." Perhaps such a position would have avoided the controversy they ended up facing—although I must say, I doubt it. As we all know, fine distinctions are difficult to maintain when controversies erupt. The difference between "sponsoring" a speech and merely "hosting" it is likely to be quickly lost once people are aroused.

After the speech was scheduled, there were still constructive steps that could have been taken that were well short of last-minute cancellation. If I were the Polish consul and I discovered, after the fact, that Tony Judt was a highly provocative and controversial figure, I would have called the sponsoring group and asked them to ensure that a balancing voice would appear on the program. This is the approach we at ADL generally favor. In the American tradition, we hold that the best remedy for "bad" speech is not censorship but *more* speech—free and open discussion that includes all points of view. We have faith that—in the long run, if not in the short term—the truth will win out, provided all sides have an equal chance to compete.

Even in the final hours before the scheduled speech by Tony Judt, a formal response could probably have been arranged. If this proved to be impossible, there was still another alternative. The Polish consulate could have announced at the start of the evening that another forum would be held in the same location within a week or two, at which an opposing point of view would be presented—and that everyone attending the Judt speech was invited to come, listen, and learn. Again, *more* speech would have been offered, and the interests of free and honest debate would have been well served.

Unfortunately, the vice consul chose none of these options. Instead, he took a step that, inevitably, looked panicky and ill-considered.

I think I understand his motivation. Realizing, at the last possible moment, that the appearance by Judt was likely to stir up a hornet's nest, Kasprzyk wanted above all to avoid having his institution swept up in controversy. As a professional diplomat, the last thing he wanted to do, I'm sure, was to create an incident that would reflect badly on his own judgment as well as on the reputation of his country. This was an especially pressing concern for Kasprzyk as a representative of Poland, a country whose international standing has been tarnished by the willing participation of some of its citizens in the Nazi-led Holocaust. Perhaps desperate to avoid further association of Poland with activities antagonistic to Israel or the Jewish people, the vice consul tried to distance himself and the consulate from Tony Judt.

Ironically, the very action he took in an attempt to shun controversy produced a controversy that proved far more nettlesome.

The controversy began with a misunderstanding. It started with Patricia S. Hutchinson, the president of Network 20/20. During the afternoon in question, she called the Polish consulate to ask about some detail related to the program for that evening. She got an assistant on the line who had seen the message our European Affairs director had left earlier: "Please call Abe Foxman at ADL." Now, my colleague had left *his* phone number, not mine; so when the vice consul returned the call, he did not speak with me. But the office assistant didn't know this. All he knew was that his boss, the vice consul, was returning the call he'd received. And so when Hutchinson called, she was told, "The vice consul can't speak with you now. He's talking with Abe Foxman of ADL."

You can see where this is heading. Later in the afternoon, when the vice consul made the decision to cancel the speech, he called Hutchinson and gave her the bad news. Hutchinson was understandably upset— and she naturally drew a connection between this decision and the (erroneous) information she'd been given earlier. It's easy to imagine what went through her mind: *Abe Foxman speaks to the vice consul—and then, two hours later, the speech is canceled! Obviously the ADL must have demanded the cancellation—and the Polish consulate gave in.*

Within hours, this interpretation of the incident was gaining wide currency. Soon everyone "knew" that this is what had happened—that ADL "pressure" had forced the Polish consulate to cancel the Tony Judt speech. Of course, what everyone "knew" was completely false. But unfortunately, in some cases, falsehood has an advantage over truth—particularly when the falsehood fits a preexisting image or narrative that some people *prefer* to believe. That was very much the case in this instance.

And so the controversy erupted. On October 4 an article appeared in the *New York Sun,* a daily newspaper, that attributed the cancellation of Judt's speech to pressure from ADL. Later, a similar story in the *Jewish Week* made the same claim. A day earlier, Tony Judt himself had sent out a "blast" e-mail to friends, colleagues, and associates, in which he wrote:

> I was due to speak this evening, in Manhattan, to a group called Network 20/20 comprising young business leaders, NGOs, academics, etc, from the US and many countries. Topic: the Israel Lobby and US Foreign Policy. The meetings are always held at the Polish Consulate in Manhattan.
>
> I just received a call from the President of Network 20/20. The talk was canceled because the Polish Consulate had been threatened by the Anti-Defamation League. Serial phone-calls from ADL President Abe Foxman warned them off hosting anything involving Tony Judt. If they persisted, he warned, he would smear the charge of Polish collaboration with anti-Israeli antisemites (= me) all over the front page of every daily paper in the city (an indirect quote). They caved and Network 20/20 were forced to cancel.
>
> Whatever your views on the Middle East I hope you find this as serious and frightening as I do. This is, or used to be, the United States of America.[12]

Polish vice consul Krzysztopf Kasprzyk was quoted in a *Washington Post* story about the controversy and specifically about the calls he received from spokespersons for Jewish organizations. "[T]he phone calls were very elegant," he supposedly said, "but may be interpreted as exercising a delicate pressure. That's obvious—we are adults and our IQs are high enough to understand that."[13]

Now all hell broke loose. Anti-Zionists, partisans of the Palestinian cause, those with unorthodox views of the Middle East that they felt hadn't gotten a fair hearing, and—yes—a few people who just happen to dislike Jews, all seized on this story as evidence of the supposed stranglehold that groups such as ADL have on the national debate. They enlisted support from well-meaning but, in some cases, naïve or uninformed academics, writers, journalists, and scholars who care deeply about freedom of speech and who assumed, based on the erroneous news reports about the Judt affair, that this freedom was now being threatened by officious members of the Israel lobby.

This widely varied coalition of concerned individuals ended up generating not one but two letters of protest aimed at me, the ADL, and the other Jewish leaders who were supposed to have orchestrated the "silencing" of Tony Judt.

The first letter, titled "A Statement in Support of Open and Free Discussion About U.S. and Israeli Foreign Policy and Against Suppression of Speech," was organized by Norman Birnbaum, an emeritus professor at Georgetown University Law Center. It specifically referred to me, the Anti-Defamation League, and several other leading Jewish American organizations as having organized and led a campaign to suppress Tony Judt's freedom of speech and thereby stifle debate about Israel. The letter began by describing a general atmosphere in which American foreign policy discussions are dominated by a single monolithic point of view. The key paragraphs stated:

Against this background [of Jewish organizations trying to "set the agenda" for American debate on the Middle East], a group of younger citizens of New York recently invited Professor Judt to open a discussion on the Israel lobby. The group usually meets at the Polish Consulate in New York. Dr. Abraham Foxman of the Anti-Defamation League took exception to the invitation and induced the Polish Consulate to deny its premises to the group. We consider this to have been an act of political vigilantism, and entirely incompatible with the culture of a democracy. . . .

Dr. Foxman has comported himself as an adversary of our traditions. His behavior is all the more regrettable, since the ultimate security of the American Jewish community depends upon the maintenance of our traditions of openness and pluralism.[14]

When it was published in *Archipelago* magazine, this letter was signed by over 150 people, mostly academics but also including some journalists, editors, think tank members, and other intellectuals.

The second letter of protest was written by Mark Lilla, a political philosopher at the University of Chicago, and Richard Sennett, a sociologist at NYU and the London School of Economics. It was published in the *New York Review of Books* together with a brief, inaccurate account of the events of October 3, which quoted the following e-mail from Tony Judt himself:

At 4:15 PM [on October 3] when [Patricia Huntington], the President [of Network 20/20] received a telephone call canceling the event scheduled to take place within the hour, she was informed that ADL President Abe Foxman was on the other line to the Consul General. We can only imagine what kind of pressure was brought to bear to prevent me from speaking on

such short notice. It was no surprise to me that I received a
call from the New York Sun within 10 minutes of the news.
The Sun must have been contacted by the ADL; who else
would do so?[15]

(For the record, we did not call the *New York Sun*.)

The letter that followed was signed by over a hundred people, including several associated with the *New Republic* magazine: the magazine's editor, Franklin Foer; two former editors, Andrew Sullivan
and Peter Beinart; and contributing editors Alan Wolfe and Leon
Wieseltier.

This letter was more temperate in its tone than the Birnbaum letter. It eschewed the inflammatory language of "political vigilantism"
and the implication that ADL had behaved in an anti-American fashion. But it, too, assumed that the ADL was responsible for the cancellation of Judt's speech. It then declared, in words addressed to the ADL
and to me personally:

> The ADL has recently been very critical of those academics and
> intellectuals, like Professor Judt, who have raised questions
> about the Israel lobby and American foreign policy, an issue on
> which reasonable people have disagreed. This does not surprise
> us or disturb us. What does surprise and disturb us is that an
> organization dedicated to promoting civil rights and public ed-
> ucation should threaten and exert pressure to cancel a lecture
> by an important scholar, as Ms. Huntington says happened.
>
> In a democracy, there is only one appropriate response to
> a lecture, article, or book one does not agree with. It is to give
> another lecture, write another article, or publish another

book. For much of its hundred-year history your organization worked side by side with other Americans who wanted to guarantee that freedom for all, and your mission statement still declares: "the goal remains the same: to stand up for the core values of America against those who seek to undermine them through word or deed."[16]

Yes, our mission statement still refers to "the core values of America"—and the ADL is still committed to defending those values. As I hope you are beginning to understand, our actions in the Tony Judt case don't conflict with that commitment at all. And, in fact, our behavior throughout was entirely consistent with the approach recommended in the Lilla letter: to openly criticize policy positions with which we disagree, and to seek to broaden the public debate rather than to narrow it or shut it down.

When I received a copy of the Lilla letter, I quickly realized that it was based on a serious misunderstanding of what had actually happened. In the interest of clearing up the misunderstanding, I contacted the lead authors and proposed that we meet to discuss the situation. I was certain that, if I had a chance to clarify the sequence of events, the issue would be defused, and all of us could devote our time and energy to more worthwhile matters. Unfortunately, my offer was rejected. Instead, I was told that the letter would soon be published in the *New York Review of Books*, and that I could respond in that forum if I chose to do so (which of course I did).

To me, this was one of the most disappointing aspects of the whole controversy. The fact that the academics behind the Lilla letter—some of them distinguished authors and scholars—refused to talk about the facts of the case before rushing into print with their accusation seems to me the antithesis of fair play. Freedom of debate is a crucial academic value that I strongly support. But don't intellectual integrity and the willingness to engage with one's adversaries deserve equal support?

As the battle was played out in the media, the real facts began to emerge—slowly and without much clarity. The Polish consulate changed its account several times. Patricia Huntington, the president of Network 20/20, contacted the *New York Sun* and the *Jewish Week* to disavow her earlier statements about the ADL having exerted pressure on the Polish consulate and asked them to correct their stories.[17]

As I've explained, I never actually called the Polish consulate to complain about the Tony Judt speech. However, it turned out that the leader of another prominent Jewish organization, David Harris of the American Jewish Committee, did call. He even told the *New York Sun* as much. Although the AJC was cited much less frequently in the press accounts than the ADL, it appears that Harris may have actually played more of a role in inspiring the consulate's decision than I did. But the fundamental truth remains that it was the Polish consulate alone that chose to cancel Tony Judt's speech. To try to place the responsibility for that ill-advised decision on some cabal of pro-Israeli groups is fairly ludicrous.

As the facts emerged, people's attitudes began to shift. Leon Wieseltier and Peter Beinart, two of the signers of the Lilla letter of protest, both criticized Tony Judt in the pages of the *New Republic*. Much of the steam seemed to leak out of the tempest-in-a-teapot of outrage over the supposed assault on free speech. Unfortunately, what remained behind was a residue of damage to the ADL's reputation, especially among people who'd heard of the Judt affair without following the story closely or to its conclusion. In the realm of public opinion—especially in these days of the ultrarapid news cycle and the ultrashort media attention span—it's much easier to besmirch an individual's or organization's reputation than to remove a stain that is undeserved.

One of the more temperate articles about the Tony Judt episode was authored by Alan Wolfe and published in the *Chronicle of Higher Education*.[18] Yet even this article reveals how badly the public understanding of this issue has been clouded by confusion, misinformation, and bias.

Like most accounts, Wolfe's article assumed that complaints that the ADL and I had sought to pressure the Polish consulate into canceling the Tony Judt speech were accurate (though Wolfe did at least acknowledge our denials of involvement, which not all writers bothered to do). Wolfe went on to link the Judt case with some other incidents in which, in Wolfe's judgment, "Jews have found themselves on the wrong side of a free-speech issue." He cited four cases: the cancellation of an art exhibit featuring paintings by Palestinian teenagers at Brandeis University; protests by some prominent Jews against the proposed offering of a professorship at Yale to Juan Cole, a Middle East scholar whose views tilt against Israel; criticism of Human Rights Watch for its accusations that Israel violated human rights during the 2006 conflict with Lebanon; and the controversy over the Walt and Mearsheimer paper, which (as Wolfe notes) led Harvard's John F. Kennedy School of Government to remove its logo from the online publication of the paper.

This was quite a grab bag of incidents, no two exactly alike. None seems truly to have been an act of censorship. In three cases (Brandeis, Yale, and Harvard), a private educational institution exercised its own judgment in deciding whether or not to lend its imprimatur and prestige to an activity or an individual deemed controversial or biased by some. It would be difficult to argue, I think, that a university is somehow *obligated* to promote people or works with which it strongly disagrees. In the fourth case (Human Rights Watch), public statements by one organization were challenged by public statements issued by other people—a perfect illustration, I would think, of the principle that speech with which one disagrees should be countered with *more* speech presenting an alternative point of view. Would Wolfe argue that those who disagreed with Human Rights Watch had a responsibility to remain silent?

Even Wolfe seemed to acknowledge that his litany of "Jewish illiberalism" didn't really amount to much:

> None of those cases resulted in the suppression of ideas: The Brandeis exhibit was moved to MIT; Cole retains his professorship at the University of Michigan at Ann Arbor, and his blog, Informed Comment, is as popular as ever; Human Rights Watch will have many opportunities in the future, alas, to document abuses by all sides in the Middle East conflict; and Walt and Mearsheimer, despite the factual errors and

sometimes hysterical tone of their working paper, received a very lucrative offer from Farrar Strauss [sic] to publish a book based upon it.[19]

This is *not* a very impressive record of success in suppressing dissent for the supposedly all-powerful Israel lobby.

As for Tony Judt himself, the outcome of the controversy over his canceled speech seems a bit ironic. The resulting furor generated many newspaper and journal articles, letters to the editor, online debates, and campus discussions, all of which made Tony Judt and his extreme positions on Israel far more famous than ever before.

As I write, the media coverage of Judt continues to flow, all tied to the Polish consulate controversy and most of it highly sympathetic. I'm looking, for example, at a lengthy interview in the prestigious *Financial Times* in which Judt comes across as the sensitive, much-aggrieved victim of a supposed "obsession with blocking any criticism of Israel"—an obsession, Judt adds, that is "uniquely American." The latter remark undoubtedly brought a smile of self-satisfaction to the lips of the *Financial Times*'s primarily British readers, as did the sad comment with which Judt concluded the interview: "I am tempted at least twice a day to go back to Europe."[20] Ah, how superior those humane, tolerant Europeans are—as opposed to us "obsessed" Americans, who merely create and support the universities, such as NYU, where Tony Judt teaches and earns his living.

Back in the 1970s, Gene Tenace, a talented outfielder with the Oakland A's, developed quite a reputation as the most underrated player in baseball. A sportswriter supposedly once asked Tenace, "How do you feel about the fact that you get so little media coverage?" Tenace replied, "Actually, I get a lot of coverage, but it's all about how little coverage I get!"

Tony Judt, it seems, has become the Gene Tenace of Middle East policy—someone whose policy views have become widely known due to the fact that they have been so ruthlessly suppressed!

So if there are winners and losers in the Judt affair, I think we have to put Tony Judt himself in the winner's column, and ADL and Abe Foxman on the losing side—at least as far as public relations success is concerned. I'll leave it to the reader to judge whether or not this outcome has been a fair or honest one.

And what about society as a whole? Has the Judt affair left American civil society more open, tolerant, wise, and thoughtful—or the reverse? Perhaps it's too soon to tell. The Judt controversy, as we've seen, is just one part of an ongoing series of battles about U.S. foreign policy, the alliance with Israel, the quest for peace in the Middle East, the role of American Jews in influencing the national debate, and, in a sense, the evolving nature of democracy itself. This conflict is being played out against a backdrop of national division and international tension that has exacerbated everyone's sensitivities and prompted a search for scapegoats, neither of which promotes healthy, constructive dialogue. Yet I have faith that, in the long run, both the people of the United States and the those throughout the democratic world will recognize and understand the facts and reject the conspiracy mongering, biased thinking, and evidence slanting that I believe characterize the Mearsheimer-Walt and Tony Judt side of the debate.

———————◆———————

I think there are some very specific lessons that fair-minded individuals can draw from the entire Judt affair, lessons that can serve us well in responding intelligently to the next controversy, whether it be an ultimately minor one like the Judt affair or—heaven forbid—a major crisis in community relationships like the Dreyfus affair in France.

- *When strong emotions are involved, intellectual honesty becomes fragile.*

I assume that most people, whether intellectuals, policy experts, or ordinary citizens, operate from a basis of good will. They seek the truth, respect the honesty and dignity of their opponents in controversy, and ultimately want to find solutions to world problems that will benefit both their own country and all humankind. (Unfortunately, there are exceptions: outright bigots, haters, liars, and deceivers with whom open conversation and free debate are really pointless. But people like these are very few in number, and once they are identified, most decent people will shun them—as they should.) When dealing with the vast majority of people who are, in fact, well-intentioned, all parties should strive to behave with intellectual honesty. Only in this way can debate lead toward the truth.

Most people, as I say, want to behave this way. But when strong emotions are involved, it's very difficult. Topics that engage powerful personal feelings—whether these are love, loyalty, and devotion or resentment, anger, and hatred—make it almost impossible for people to consider facts dispassionately, evaluate information fairly, and draw conclusions without bias.

Unfortunately, Israel and the quest for peace in the Middle East generate extremely strong emotions which often push people in opposite directions. This makes open debate centered on the search for truth extremely difficult. People who are deeply committed to a particular point of view find it incredibly hard not to see their opponents and all the facts associated with them through the prism of their disagreement. Jumping to conclusions, begging the questions, cutting corners in argument, and oversimplification become almost overpowering temptations.

This problematic tendency on the part of human beings came to the fore in the Judt affair. When the Polish consulate canceled Judt's appearance, it was all too easy for Judt and all those who share his perspective to assume that, of course, pressure from the ADL and Abe Foxman must have been to blame. It was a narrative that fit all too comfortably into their preconceived notions about the ADL, the Israel Lobby, and the power of American Jews. Indeed, it would have been almost impossible for them *not* to assume the worst about me. And so—in defiance of the facts—that is exactly what they did. In fact, in an email dated October 6, 2006 to Peter Beinart and "past participants of Remarque Forum," with a copy sent to as many as one hundred academics, journalists, writers, and diplomats, Judt described me as a "lying bigot" and a "Fascist."

Overcoming this human tendency is a terribly difficult thing to do. I know, because I have had to work so hard on it myself. As national director of the ADL, I frequently have to monitor, evaluate, and pass judgment on accusations of bigotry, bias, or outright anti-Semitism on the part of people and organizations, whether well known or obscure. This process involves a constant struggle on my part to overcome any bias or prejudice I may have.

When I get a phone call or an e-mail saying, "Have you heard about the hateful behavior that's being reported about So-and-so?" I often have an immediate, visceral reaction, either positive or negative. If the person mentioned is someone I happen to know, and perhaps even consider a friend, my first thought may be to deny and defend. If the person is someone about whom I may have a negative feeling— perhaps a politician whose policies I disagree with, or even an actor or talk show host whose persona rubs me the wrong way—my first reaction may be to criticize or condemn. Either way, I've learned to distrust those snap reactions. The worst thing I can do is to act on them.

Instead, I must start by verifying the facts, either in person or through a trusted researcher. If I can hear or see the words or deeds and evaluate them myself, so much the better. Then I must put the facts into a broader context, including the time, occasion, and situation in which the events happened, the background and history of the person involved, extenuating circumstances that might cause an action to be overinterpreted or misunderstood, and the person's response to any immediate complaints or charges that have been expressed. Finally, I often seek out the individual for a personal conversation in which I can have an opportunity to better understand where he or she is coming from, what was intended by the offensive words or deeds, and whether they reflect true bigotry and hatred or, as is often the case, simple ignorance, carelessness, or a momentary lapse in judgment.

Only after working through this process am I in any position to pass judgment on another human being, especially publicly. And even then, of course, I know I may be wrong—and must be prepared to rescind my judgment when it has been shown to be mistaken. Humility and continual self-examination are crucial components of the process. If I carry it through with diligence and patience, an intellectually honest result is likely to emerge—one that is fair and stands the test of time.

I would submit that, if my critics in the Judt affair had taken the time to evaluate the events in the way I've described above, the situation might never have become such a source of bitter—and ultimately needless—acrimony.

- *Clear distinctions must be drawn as to what does and does not constitute "censorship."*

A distressing element of the Judt affair has been the readiness of many people to cry "censorship" when confronted with criticism of their own point of view. Because our society has such a strong commitment to freedom of speech—a commitment I share, of course—this accusation is particularly powerful, and is often enough to silence those who might otherwise speak out against messages they consider hateful. I think this is a serious mistake and a grave misuse of the word "censorship" itself.

Properly understood, "censorship" applies only to government control of the content of speech. When a government agency must issue licenses to publishers before books or newspapers may be printed; when a government employee must approve the language used in news broadcasts before they go on the air; when government permits are required before public speeches or political demonstrations may take place—all of these are rightly denounced as acts of censorship, and no society that operates in this fashion can truly be called free.

In our capitalist society, the word "censorship" can also be extended to describe unwarranted, invasive acts of control over the content of news, entertainment, and information media by the corporations that own those media. When just a handful of large companies own a major share of the publishers, broadcasters, and other content providers, there's a real danger that corporate interference in the choices made by editors, producers, writers, and other content experts may severely limit the information citizens receive and the types of public debate they witness and participate in.

I don't refer, in this case, to such forms of content control as, for example, a TV network's refusal to air programming that is patently offensive to almost everyone in the audience and without redeeming cultural or social importance. I think we can agree that this would be an act of simple business judgment that is understandable and appropriate. Instead, I'm referring to blanket attempts to restrict a large swath of the media to one or a few "acceptable" points of view, or to exclude significant facts and ideas because of objections by corporate leaders.

In practice, the lines between these two forms of control can be hard to define, and the rules need to be constantly scrutinized and debated. But, my point is that only the most sweeping, rigid, and politically motivated form of corporate control of content ought to be tarred with the powerful word "censorship."

Thus, censorship does *not* apply when a private organization (whether a newspaper, a publisher, or record company, or a university) decides not to present, endorse, support, or promote a particular message with which it disagrees.

It does *not* apply when an individual or a group expresses disapproval of messages presented by some other individual or group, even if that disapproval is expressed in strong terms or using vehement, forceful symbolism—for example, by picketing outside a lecture hall.

It does *not* apply when individuals or groups choose to withdraw their financial participation or other support for an institution that presents a message they disagree with—for example, when board members resign from the leadership of a museum that mounts an exhibit they consider offensive.

It does *not* apply when individuals or groups urge others to shun, avoid, or refuse to patronize another individual or group that presents a message they find offensive. Thus, if a college student walks out in protest during a commencement address and invites other students to join him, that action may or may not be an appropriate response to the speaker's message—but it is *not* censorship.

Freedom of speech is about the tumult of ideas, freely exchanged and often conflicting, even when those ideas may challenge, anger, and antagonize others. None of us can claim the freedom to go through life without being offended. The willingness to respond to offenses, not with calls for suppression but with language that exhibits and demonstrates respect, is one hallmark of a civilized society.

So let's not be quick to censor others—and by the same token, let's not be quick to cry "Censorship!" just because we don't like the criticism that we're receiving at the hands of others. Either mistake is a violation of the real spirit of freedom.

- *A single standard by which to define legitimate and illegitimate criticism must be sought and consistently applied.*

One of the most often-repeated canards in the entire Judt affair is the accusation that members of the Israel Lobby as well as other defenders of Israel are quick to conflate criticism of Israel with anti-Semitism. It's an accusation I deny. Are there some overly sensitive Jews who are excessively prone to seeing anti-Semitism where none really exists? There probably are. But I don't agree that this charge applies to me, to the Anti-Defamation League, or to the great majority of Jewish leaders and Jewish organizations with which I'm acquainted. We know the difference between criticism of Israel and anti-Semitism, and we are careful to respect that difference.

The biggest challenge, I think, arises in trying to draw the distinction between criticism of Israel that is fair and legitimate and criticism that crosses the line into bigotry, bias, and—yes—anti-Semitism. How would I define this line of legitimacy? I think there are several criteria to consider.

I think criticism that faults specific Israeli policies and proposes realistic alternatives—even if I might disagree with those alternatives—is legitimate. On the other hand, criticism that condemns Israel *simply for existing* and implies that the only way Israel can satisfy its critics is by disappearing is *not* legitimate.

I think criticism that finds fault with Israel on the basis of rules or principles that are generally accepted by all nations and applied evenhandedly—even if I might disagree with those principles and their application to Israel—is legitimate. On the other hand, criticism that singles out Israel for behavior that many other countries engage in without suffering any reproach is *not* legitimate.

I think criticism that considers realistically the dangers, difficulties, and risks Israel faces due to its position in the world, and that evaluates the motives and decisions made by its people and its leaders on that basis—even if I might disagree with the conclusions reached by such an evaluation—is legitimate. On the other hand, criticism that ignores every problem Israel faces, assumes that its people and leaders can accomplish anything they desire instantly and without difficulty, and therefore concludes that only bad faith or evil motives can explain any failure or error on Israel's part is *not* legitimate.

Do you think I'm quibbling? I don't believe so. If the distinctions I'm drawing seem arcane or legalistic, try to put yourself in the place of an Israel being criticized in ways I've defined as illegitimate. Would you want yourself—or a group or a country that you identify with and love—to be judged on that basis? How would you feel about a political "expert" declaring that a country you love should not even *exist?* How would you feel about having that country attacked and condemned for doing the same things that dozens of other countries do—and are often praised for doing? How would you feel about having that country's leaders treated as if they are *by definition* untrustworthy, dishonest bad actors? Wouldn't such treatment feel unfair, unjust, bigoted?

I think that everyone who is concerned about bringing peace to the Middle East owes it to themselves to perform this act of self-projection into the shoes of a supporter of Israel. Before you condemn the country or its leaders, try honestly to imagine being in their position. What sacrifices would *you* be willing to make for peace? How vulnerable would you be willing to make your country and its people?

And, yes, it's equally essential that Israelis and supporters of Israel around the world be willing to make a similar mental projection into the minds and experiences of Arabs in the Palestinian territories. Their fears, dreams, resentments, and hopes must be recognized and understood by their Jewish counterparts. Mutual understanding and respect among all the peoples of the Middle East is an essential step toward the open, realistic dialogue we need if a true and lasting peace is to be achieved.

Meanwhile, however, the unwillingness of many leaders in the Arab world and their sympathizers and supporters in the West to grant even a modicum of respect to the concerns of the people of Israel poses a significant barrier to peace. We have seen Israel receive biased and unfair treatment repeatedly in public debates, in the world media, and in international forums. The pattern is so egregious and so unmistakable that we are at a loss to explain it, except by assuming there must be some strong motive behind it. And this is why, in our judgment, criticism of Israel that is intensely biased, unfair, and illogical is driven by something more despicable, less defensible, less innocent than simple misunderstanding or difference of opinion. In extreme cases, the only word we can apply is anti-Semitism.

Is there a difference between criticism of Israel and anti-Semitism? You bet there is, and I've just defined it. I defy anyone to claim that I equate the two.

5

A PRESIDENT LOSES HIS WAY

FORMER PRESIDENT JIMMY CARTER IS, IN MANY WAYS, A good man—of that, there can be little doubt. He loves his family. His lifelong marriage to his wife Rosalynn is, by all accounts, a true partnership of minds and spirits as well as a love match. He appears to be (as far as any outsider can judge) a serious and devoted member of his faith. And in the public sphere, President Carter has done much that is admirable. His volunteer work for organizations like Habitat for Humanity has placed a welcome focus on the needs of the poorest among us. The efforts of the Carter Center to eradicate terrible diseases like river blindness and guinea worm in

Africa and elsewhere in the developing world have saved and improved countless lives. And President Carter has worked tirelessly to promote peace and democracy through his efforts as a freelance diplomat and an election monitor. In all these ways, President Carter has earned the accolade so often bestowed upon him: "The greatest *former* president in American history."

All true. And yet . . . there is this blind spot. A disturbing blind spot that tarnishes the otherwise admirable legacy of this well-meaning, deeply caring man. A terrible blind spot that even threatens to overshadow much of the good that Jimmy Carter has done, by making his honored name a tool in the hands of people who stand for everything that Jimmy Carter abhors: hatred, intolerance, violence.

When a good man makes a serious error in judgment, the impact can sometimes be even worse than that of the outright crimes committed by bad people.

There are avowed anti-Semites active in the world today, as there have been for centuries. A few have the potential to achieve great power and thereby endanger the freedom and safety of millions of people (a handful currently control the government of Iran, for example). We must take the threat posed by people like these very seriously.

But most of the outright anti-Semites of today are relatively harmless. They occupy the fringes of society and are largely ignored in serious debates. They rarely get a forum in the mainstream media or at top-flight universities or among leading politicians.

The graver danger to the public discourse comes from good men such as Jimmy Carter—a good man with a disturbing blind spot that leads him to say things whose deeper meaning he may scarcely understand, words that lend the authority and respect earned by his once-high office and by his admirable accomplishments to ideas that are not only despicable but downright dangerous.

It's painful to have to publicly criticize a man like Jimmy Carter. But truth is truth, falsehood is falsehood, and the difference between the two must be honored. Because there is nothing quite as dangerous as a falsehood that is being spread by the words and deeds of an otherwise good man.

———————◆———————

What forces me to focus in this book on the dangerous blind spot of Jimmy Carter is the presence on the *New York Times* best-seller list of the former president's most recent and most controversial book. This slim volume, a highly personal discourse on the ongoing conflict in the Middle East, was greeted with outrage and dismay by friends of Israel as soon as it was published. Many, many others, however, have embraced the book and its message, as evidenced not only by its months atop many other best-seller lists but also by the hundreds of laudatory messages found, for example, on the Amazon book-selling website. Clearly, the book has struck a nerve—and for that reason alone it deserves serious and thoughtful scrutiny.

The immediate outcry that greeted President Carter's book was based in part on its title—*Palestine: Peace Not Apartheid.* Is this an example of exaggerated Israeli (or Jewish) sensitivity—a silly fuss about "mere" semantics? I don't think so. Let me explain why.

The word "apartheid" has a very specific meaning and history. It is a word in the South African language known as Afrikaans that describes the system of racial segregation enforced in South Africa from 1948 to 1994. Apartheid was designed to form a legal framework for perpetual economic and political dominance of black South Africans by people of European descent. Under apartheid, people were legally classified into racial groups, the main ones being Black, White, Coloured, and Asian (consisting of Indians and Pakistanis), and were geographically and forcibly separated from each other on the basis of the legal classification. The black majority, in particular, legally became citizens of particular "homelands" ("Bantustans") that were nominally sovereign nations but were operated much like the Indian reservations in the United States and the Aboriginal Reserves in Canada and Australia—second-class enclaves where relatively powerless people were forced to live together, often in abject poverty.

Apartheid was justly reviled throughout the world as a racist system reminiscent of the Nazis. By the late 1980s, it was the target of international sanctions and a powerful divestiture movement that exerted enormous economic and political pressure on the South African regime. In the early 1990s the apartheid regime was gradually abolished, and in 1994 majority rule was finally introduced in the country.

For Jimmy Carter to use the word "apartheid" in reference to the Palestinian territories is a deliberate act of provocation, an attempt to create controversy by drawing an analogy between the system of oppression created by white South Africans and the way in which Palestinian Arabs are treated today by Israel. And in a world where Israel is often accused of being a racist society, Carter's charge plays into the hands of those who accuse Israel of being an apartheid society.

On all levels, the comparison is simply factually and historically invalid. An excellent summary of the realities on the ground in Israel today and how they do or do not compare to the apartheid era in South Africa was published by journalist Benjamin Pogrund under the revealing title "Apartheid? Israel Is a Democracy in Which Arabs Vote." Pogrund knows whereof he speaks. A Jewish native of South Africa, he fought against the apartheid regime before moving to Jerusalem, where he now lives and works on efforts to reconcile Jewish and Muslim people in Israel.

In his article, Pogrund candidly acknowledges that Arabs, who constitute some twenty percent of the current population of Israel, are subject to discrimination. They hold fewer civil service jobs than Jews, attend schools that are less well funded, and sometimes have difficulty getting jobs or owning land. These forms of mistreatment are deplorable, and, as Pogrund points out, they have been intensely criticized by many in Israel, both Arabs and Jews. But do they amount to a system of segregation that deserves the name "apartheid"? Here is Pogrund's assessment:

Under apartheid, remember, no detail of life was immune to discrimination by law. Skin colour determined every single person's life, literally from birth until death: where you were born, where you went to school, what job you had, which bus you used, what park bench you sat on and in which cemetery you were buried. In Israel, discrimination occurs despite equality in law; it is extensive, it is buttressed by custom, but it is not remotely comparable with the South African panoply of discrimination enforced by parliamentary legislation. The difference is fundamental.[1]

Pogrund goes on to demonstrate the enormous difference between Israel today and South Africa under apartheid with these personal observations:

> Two years ago I had major surgery in a Jerusalem hospital: the surgeon was Jewish, the anaesthetist was Arab, the doctors and nurses who looked after me were Jews and Arabs. Jews and Arabs share meals in restaurants and travel on the same trains, buses and taxis, and visit each other's homes.
>
> Could any of this possibly have happened under apartheid? Of course not.

Are there instances of discrimination and unequal treatment in Israel? Unfortunately, yes, as in many countries, including the United States. But it is *not* a system deeply embedded in either Israel's Basic Laws or its psyche. Arabs in Israel today are speaking up for their rights, pursuing legal redress through the courts, and in many instances winning their cases. That's as it should be. And it could never have happened under apartheid.

Confronted with facts like these during interviews subsequent to his book's publication, President Carter has defended himself by claiming that he never intended to apply the word "apartheid" to daily life within Israel. His intention, rather, was to describe the difficulties of life for Palestinian Arabs in the territories. In these enclaves, Carter asserts, the network of Israeli settlements, interconnecting roads, military checkpoints, and barriers separates Palestinians from one another and from the outside world, making them virtual prisoners in their own homes and limiting their economic and social opportunities. It is this situation, Carter claims, that deserves the epithet of "apartheid" used in his book's title.

If you haven't read Carter's book, you might wonder why it has been necessary for him to explain away the meaning of its title in press interviews. Surely, one might think, the book itself would fully and clearly explain the title, making explicit exactly what the author meant and didn't mean by it? One might think so, but the book is remarkably careless in its use of this explosive and denigrating term. (It is also very sketchily sourced, devoid of footnotes, bibliography, or any other scholarly apparatus, seemingly relying on the author's personal notes and recollections for almost all of its content.) The feeling one gets is that Carter used the word without much awareness of its explosive quality and perhaps without thinking through its implications. As journalist Joseph Lelyveld pointed out in a thoughtful review, "Carter alludes to apartheid only glancingly in his text, touching on the subject in just four paragraphs in the entire book, adding up to barely a couple of pages. . . . he leaves it to readers to fill in the blanks in his argument."[2]

It's stunning that a former president who prides himself on his literary output should be so offhand in his use of such powerfully charged language. In any case, what about Carter's narrower and perhaps more defensible argument—that Israel, while not a full-fledged "apartheid regime," does impose a set of restrictions on Palestinians in the territories that could be compared to South Africa's treatment of nonwhites?

This is a more difficult case. But any fair analysis of the facts must conclude that, here, too, Jimmy Carter is guilty of rhetorical overkill. Yes, the conditions under which the Palestinian Arabs live are deplorable. However, it must be said that the Palestinians, by rejecting Israeli peace offers and by employing terror and violence, are at least significantly responsible for their own condition. The territories are just that—lands captured in wars that Israel fought in its own defense and that it now holds until some just and peaceful way of transferring them to other control can be found.

There is no joy to living in occupied lands. In such conditions, everyone suffers, and the sufferings of the Palestinians can't and shouldn't be minimized.

But does that mean that conditions in the West Bank amount to apartheid? Not at all. Consider: The *avowed purposes* of South Africa's apartheid system were to establish permanent rule by whites of European descent over native blacks; to exploit nonwhite peoples as a source of cheap forced labor; and to prevent them from ever having a say in the governance of their own country.

None of these purposes obtains in Israel *or* in the West Bank today. The Jews of Israel don't want to rule the Palestinians—they want to live apart from them, in a country of their own, where Jews are a majority and Jewish culture and religion are taken as the norm.

The Jews have no desire to exploit the Palestinians as a work force; in fact, one of the most bitter complaints of many Palestinians concerns the difficulty they experience in applying for well-paying jobs in Israel and traveling to workplaces there.

And the Jews of Israel aren't interested in suppressing Palestinian self-rule. The day when the Palestinian Arabs establish truly democratic rule over their own homeland will be celebrated almost as joyfully in Israel as in Palestine itself. A free and democratic Palestinian state, Israelis hope, will be able to concentrate on building its own future of prosperity and peace and will no longer feel the need to attack its neighbor Israel.

So is it fair to imply that the Jews of Israel are in the same position vis-à-vis the Palestinian Arabs as the whites of South Africa vis-à-vis the blacks? In no way. Far from desiring permanent control over the Palestinians, most Israelis consider their mutual entanglement in the territories a source of frustration, danger, anxiety, and embarrassment, from which both parties will someday be delighted to be freed. And the sooner it happens, the better. Again, Carter's implied analogy—in the title of his book, no less—is simply inaccurate and libelous.

South African apartheid was so hateful, in part, because it was built on a racist ideology—precisely the same kind of ideology that gave rise to the Nazi regime and produced the unequalled horrors of the Holocaust. To accuse Israel of erecting an apartheid system is especially odious because it, in effect, equates the country's Jewish leaders with the hatemongers of Hitler's Germany, the very people whose slaughter of six million Jews helped spur the creation of Israel in the first place.

Even President Carter, who so facilely used the word "apartheid" to discuss Israel, is driven by the facts to admit that this equation is hopelessly flawed. In his own book, he writes, "The driving purpose for the forced separation of the two peoples [in the occupied territories] is unlike that in South Africa—not racism, but the acquisition of land."[3]

It's a lame confession, on more than one score. First of all, despite Carter's unsupported assertion, the real motivation of Israeli leaders for the strict controls they've instituted in and around the territories is not the acquisition of land but rather the desire to achieve security—to forestall the continuing attacks by suicide bombers and other Palestinian terrorists on Israeli civilians.

Even more important, Carter's own distinction destroys any validity the analogy to apartheid might otherwise have had. Apartheid was an invidious legal system of ethnic discrimination motivated by racial hatred. None of these characteristics—especially the crucial driving force of racism—applies in today's Palestinian-Israeli conflict. So why apply the word in the first place? Why torture the language by twisting a word into a context where it doesn't belong, only to have to explain, justify, reframe, distinguish, and clarify it after the fact?

The motivation behind this choice of words is genuinely puzzling.

It almost appears that President Carter feels driven by some unacknowledged resentment of Israel or the Jews. How else to explain his going out of his way to insult Israel by using a term that he himself acknowledges is imprecise and ultimately inaccurate? As Joseph Lelyveld comments, "to equate Israel with white South Africa of the apartheid era amounts to saying the Jewish state has no legitimacy at all."[4] And that means the use of the term goes beyond the bounds of ordinary criticism and into the realm where bias and bigotry bleed, inevitably, into anti-Semitism.

Unfortunately, the problems with President Carter's book go far beyond the title.

In its structure, *Palestine: Peace Not Apartheid* is a curious hybrid, partly an essay on American policy in the Middle East, partly a memoir of Carter's personal interactions with political leaders from the region, partly an attempt at a history of the Arab-Israeli conflict since the founding of the Jewish State.

Of course, Carter is entitled to offer any policy prescriptions he likes, and critics are free to point out their weaknesses. He is certainly free to say what he wants about his impressions of Arab and Israeli leaders, and observers who have met practically all the major players in the region are free to comment on what we consider to be Carter's misunderstandings and errors of judgment in this area.

But when it comes to history, that's a different matter. Here we move from the realm of subjective opinions into the realm of objective realities. As the late U.S. Senator Patrick Moynihan famously remarked, "You're entitled to your own opinion, but you're not entitled to your own facts."

Unfortunately, President Carter's fame and the popularity of his best-selling books mean that many thousands of readers who peruse *Palestine: Peace Not Apartheid* will probably assume that his version of the history of the modern Middle East is accurate. That is simply not so. Instead, it is riddled with errors of both commission and omission. Most distressingly, all the errors run in one direction, inevitably suggesting some bias, conscious or unconscious, on the part of the author. Carter has somehow chosen to mention and emphasize every blameworthy act on the part of the Israelis and to ignore or to minimize many such acts on the part of their Arab and Palestinian adversaries.

In a time of Islamic extremism running rampant; of suicide bombs threatening cities in Europe, Asia, and the Middle East; of Iran publicly stating its desire to wipe Israel off the map and building a nuclear weapons program to achieve that end; and of ongoing missile and rocket attacks by Hezbollah and Hamas on Israel—in a time like this, it's shocking that Carter can write as if Israel alone is the party responsible for conflict between Israel and the Palestinians.

Carter concludes: "Israel's continued control and colonization of Palestinian land have been *the primary obstacles* to a comprehensive peace agreement in the Holy Land." And, "*The bottom line is this:* Peace will come to Israel and the Middle East only when the Israeli government is willing to comply with international law, with the road map for peace . . ." [emphases added].[5]

In order to reach such a simplistic and distorted view of the struggle for peace in the region, Carter has to ignore or downplay the continuing examples of Palestinians' rejection of Israel and their terrorism, which have been part of the equation from before the founding of the nation and which, sadly, are as strong as ever today. He also has to minimize, ignore, or harshly criticize every one of Israel's peace offers and unilateral withdrawals from territories, including specifically former Israeli Prime Minister Ehud Barak's initiative at Camp David in 2000, Prime Minister Ariel Sharon's disengagement from Gaza in 2005, and current Prime Minister Ehud Olmert's campaign pledge to withdraw from the West Bank. And, he has to frame every example of Palestinian distress as simply the product of Israeli repression while ignoring the impact of many other factors, including neglect or outright hostility from Arab neighbors, well-documented corruption and self-dealing by Palestinian leaders, and the obvious need for physical security created by violent Palestinian extremism.

Even the most casual observer of world events can recognize that the issues in the prolonged Palestinian-Israeli conflict are a lot more complicated than Carter admits. It's sadly revealing that, at a time when even many Arab leaders are beginning to acknowledge how destructive and dangerous the policies of the Palestinians have been, Carter soft-pedals these issues while repeatedly condemning the Israelis for their supposed intransigence.

I don't mean to imply that Carter ignores Palestinian rejection-ism, hatred, violence, and terrorism altogether. Sometimes these his-torical realities simply can't be ignored, even by an author who is bending over backward to do just that. But when he is forced by the flow of his narrative to mention instances of such things, he refers to them in a startlingly matter-of-fact tone, as if his emotions are basi-cally disengaged. Here's a typical paragraph, in this case describing events during the U.S. presidential administration of Bill Clinton:

> Unfortunately for the peace process, Palestinian terrorists car-ried out two lethal suicide bombings in March 1996, a few weeks after the Palestinian election. Thirty-two Israeli citizens were killed, an act that probably gave the Likud's hawkish candidate, Binyamin Netanyahu, a victory over Prime Minis-ter Shimon Peres. The new leader of Israel promised never to exchange land for peace. Foreign Minister Ariel Sharon de-clared the Oslo Agreement to be "national suicide" and stated, "Everybody has to move, run and grab as many hilltops as they can to enlarge the settlements because everything we take now will stay ours. . . . Everything we don't grab will go to them." This policy precipitated Israel's tightened hold on the occupied territories and aroused further violence from the Palestinians.[6]

What a strange paragraph. The suicide bombings that killed thirty-two innocent civilians are mentioned almost casually, and Carter expresses regret not for the horrific and senseless loss of life but for the unfortunate impact he feels it had on the subsequent Israeli election. He expounds at some length on what he views as the Israeli government's excessive reaction to the Palestinian violence (the attack he mentions is, of course, only one small instance of this violence), throwing in a quotation from two years later (1998) which was not, contrary to Carter's implication, an official statement of government policy but rather a remark made at a political party gathering. And he concludes by saying that "This policy . . . aroused further violence from the Palestinians," as if to imply that terrorism is the inevitable, indeed natural and understandable, response to conflict over control of disputed lands between two competing groups.

This strange tone—treating Palestinian crimes as mere statistics while discoursing extensively on Israeli "overreactions"—is characteristic of the entire book. On page after page, acts of violence and terrorism, refusals to acknowledge the legitimacy of Israel, and statements of hatred directed toward Israelis and Jews in general by both Palestinians and others throughout the Arab world—all these are mentioned only briefly, as if they are to be taken for granted. By contrast, Israeli acts that Carter condemns, such as the expansion of settlements in the West Bank or the construction of security barriers to prevent terrorist attacks, are described in vivid detail, at great length, and characterized as serious roadblocks to peace. It's as if only the Israelis should be held to a high standard of moral and ethical conduct.

The point isn't that every Palestinian act that Carter glosses over should be furiously condemned. Nor is it that every Israeli act that Carter criticizes should be defended. As in most conflicts, there have been rights and wrongs on both sides, and there is plenty of room for open debate about how the blame should be apportioned—and, more important, about the best way forward. But any historical discussion that pretends to be objective should balance both parties on the same moral scales, something Carter conspicuously fails to do.

Carter's bias isn't revealed only in matters of tone. It is also exposed by the book's many factual errors. To illustrate, consider Carter's misrepresentation of the views and positions taken by Israeli leaders with whom he has had differences of opinion. The leading example, perhaps, is Menachem Begin, prime minister of Israel from 1977 to 1983 and cowinner with Egypt's Anwar Sadat of the 1978 Nobel Peace Prize for his role in signing the Camp David Accords.

Jimmy Carter, of course, deserves enormous credit for his work in making the Camp David Accords possible. We must never forget that it was during the Carter administration that the single greatest stride toward a comprehensive peace settlement between Israel and its Arab neighbors was taken. But it's clear, both from Carter's own accounts and from the reminiscences of other participants and observers, that in Carter's eyes the lion's share of the credit for the peace treaty between Egypt and Israel goes to Sadat (and to Carter himself), with very little left over for Begin.

Personal feelings undoubtedly play a role in Carter's assessment. Presidents, prime ministers, and diplomats are first and foremost human beings, and all human beings have their likes and dislikes. It's not a crime that Jimmy Carter doesn't have a personal fondness for Menachem Begin. But it's highly unfortunate that Carter's admiration for Sadat, and his corresponding mistrust for and dislike of Begin, should now be coloring the historical record, leading to outright factual distortions in Carter's book.

Perhaps the most serious of these distortions relates to the Israeli settlements in the West Bank. Carter has long claimed that, at the time of the Camp David negotiations, Begin had made some sort of commitment *not* to expand these settlements beyond the relative handful then in existence. In subsequent years, when the settlements were in fact expanded, Carter took this as a personal betrayal by Begin. Carter's anger over this issue simmers just under the surface of the book—for example, in his account of a meeting between the two men in 1983:

> It was no secret that Begin and I had strong public disagreements concerning the interpretation of the Camp David Accords and Israel's recent invasion of Lebanon. Unfortunately, these disputes had resulted in some personal differences as well.
>
> Now we were together again, and as had always been my custom, I expressed myself with frankness on some of the more controversial issues. . . . as he [Begin] sat without looking at me, I explained again why we believed he had not honored a commitment made during the peace negotiations to withdraw Israeli forces and to refrain from building new Israeli settlements in the West Bank. . . .
>
> He responded with just a few words in a surprisingly perfunctory manner and made it plain that our conversation should be concluded.[7]

Someone unfamiliar with the history might assume that Begin was treating the ex-president with surprising rudeness. The Israeli's attitude becomes more understandable when we consider the fact that *Begin had made no such commitment concerning the West Bank settlements.*

Historian Kenneth Stein of Emory University is a former close associate of President Carter. From 1983 to 1986, he served as the first permanent executive director of the Carter Center, and after stepping down from that post, he was the center's Middle East fellow, a position he retained until December 2006. Thus, he is especially well placed to expose the distortions in Carter's book. In considering this part of the story, Stein explains,

> During his tenure as prime minister, Begin forbade the negotiation agenda to include the West Bank and those portions of Jerusalem that the Israeli government annexed after the 1967 Six-Day War. This refusal to negotiate became Carter's core disagreement with Begin. . . . With Begin not offering a fall-back position, Carter could not initiate a conclusive Israeli-Palestinian negotiating process. He never forgave Begin.[8]

So Begin refused *from the outset* to make any commitment regarding settlements on the West Bank—a stance that President Carter disagreed with and deeply resented.

One might or might not fault Begin for his position on the West Bank settlements. Many observers agree with Carter that Israeli settlements on land that, under most proposed peace agreements, will ultimately become part of a Palestinian state have complicated the negotiating process. Carter may wish that Begin had taken a position on this issue more to his liking. But it's simply inexcusable to claim falsely that he *did* take such a position and then accuse him of deliberately reneging on an agreement.

Whereas Carter is quick to interpret Israeli actions in the worst possible light, he is all too ready to forgive, excuse, overlook, or even deny actions on the part of the Palestinians and their Arab supporters that have thrown roadblocks in the way of peace. One way in which he does this is by repeatedly quoting the words of Palestinian and Arab spokesmen making false or misleading statements of fact and then failing to challenge or correct them. As a result, the uninformed reader is led to assume that the false statements are true and that Carter is personally vouching for them.

Here are some other examples of Carter's factual carelessness in *Palestine: Peace Not Apartheid* that are cited by Kenneth Stein.

Carter describes a March 1990, meeting with Syrian President Assad over the status of the Golan Heights, a disputed territory currently controlled by Israel but claimed by Syria.[9] Stein attended that meeting and kept detailed notes. They indicate that Assad flatly rejected the notion of a demilitarized Golan Heights, saying, "we cannot accept this because we are sacrificing our sovereignty." But Carter's account suggests just the opposite. As Stein explains:

> Carter reworded the conversation to suggest that Assad was flexible and the Israelis were not. . . . This was not a slip of memory for Carter; Carter received a full set of my notes of

the March 1990 trip after its conclusion. These were inten-
tional distortions.[10]

Carter also recounts a conversation during January 2006, with Dr.
Mahmoud Ramahi, a member of the Palestinian terrorist group
Hamas:

> When I questioned him about the necessity for Hamas to re-
> nounce violence and recognize Israel, he responded that they
> had not committed an act of violence since a cease-fire was
> declared in August 2004 and were willing and able to extend
> and enforce that cease-fire (hudna) for "two, ten, or fifty
> years"—if Israel would reciprocate by refraining from attacks
> on Palestinians.[11]

Except, as Kenneth Stein points out, "Hamas on many subsequent oc-
casions claimed responsibility for firing Qassam rockets into Israel
and also claimed responsibility for the kidnapping of Gilad Shalit in
June 2006."[12] Unfortunately, you won't find Jimmy Carter setting the
record straight.

Distortions of the historical record like these, all leaning in one
direction, help to explain why historians like Stein have responded to
Carter's book with dismay. In December 2006, Stein resigned from
the advisory board of the Carter Center, citing his unhappiness over
Palestine: Peace Not Apartheid as the reason. One month later, four-
teen other members of the board followed suit. In their public letter
of resignation, they told the former president, "You have clearly aban-

doned your historic role of broker in favor of becoming an advocate for one side."[13]

Perhaps the most significant example of how *Palestine: Peace Not Apartheid* distorts the facts of history involves the attempt at forging a peace settlement between Israel and the Palestinians during the last months of the Clinton administration. (As we've seen, John Mearsheimer and Stephen Walt are also guilty of rewriting this history in their essay on "The Israel Lobby.") Eager to burnish his presidential legacy with a triumph for peace at the negotiating table, Bill Clinton worked hard at developing a compromise two-state plan that could satisfy both Palestinian demands for a homeland and the Israeli need for secure, defensible borders.

What unfolded during 2000 and the early weeks of 2001 was an important episode in the recent history of the Middle East. Unfortunately, Carter's very sketchy (eight-page) account of what happened is seriously inaccurate. We can glimpse the nature of the inaccuracy by starting with what might be called the case of the mislabeled maps.

On a page in Carter's book are two maps, one labeled "Palestinian Interpretation of Clinton's Proposal 2000" and the other, "Israeli Interpretation of Clinton's Proposal 2000." Unfortunately, both labels are incorrect, as stated in an op-ed article by no less an authority than Dennis Ross, President Clinton's envoy to the Middle East and the primary architect of the administration's proposal. As Ross explains:

The problem is that the "Palestinian interpretation" is actually taken from an *Israeli* map presented during the Camp David

summit meeting in July 2000, while the "Israeli interpretation" is an approximation of what President Clinton subsequently proposed in December of that year. Without knowing
this, the reader is left to conclude that the Clinton proposals
must have been so ambiguous and unfair that Yasir Arafat, the
Palestinian leader, was justified in rejecting them. But that is
simply untrue. . . .

It is certainly legitimate to debate whether President Clinton's proposal could have settled the conflict. It is not legitimate, however, to rewrite history and misrepresent what the
Clinton ideas were.[14]

Indeed, Carter clearly pins the blame for the failure of the Clinton initiative on Israeli intransigence. Here is Carter's summary:

A new round of talks was held at Taba [Egypt] in January
2001, during the last few days of the Clinton presidency, between President Arafat and the Israeli foreign minister, and it
was later claimed that the Palestinians rejected a "generous
offer" put forward by Prime Minister Barak with Israel keeping only 5 percent of the West Bank. *The fact is that no such offers were ever made* [emphasis added]. Barak later said, "It was
plain to me that there was no chance of reaching a settlement
at Taba. Therefore I said there would be no negotiations and
there would be no delegation and there would be official discussions and no documentation. Nor would Americans be
present in the room. The only thing that took place at Taba
were non-binding contacts between senior Israelis and senior
Palestinians."

The election of Ariel Sharon as prime minister two months
later brought an end to these efforts to find accommodation.[15]

Notice what Carter is trying to do here. By insisting that no serious Israeli offer was ever made, he is depicting the Palestinians as willing negotiating partners and the Israelis as stubborn and uninvolved.

The facts say otherwise. Detailed accounts by the two men most deeply involved in the ongoing negotiations—envoy Dennis Ross and President Bill Clinton himself—both flatly contradict Carter's version of events. I'll focus on Clinton's memoirs. They describe a series of Israeli proposals, each hammered out through tough negotiations between Prime Minister Ehud Barak and Clinton—and each short-sightedly shot down by Yasser Arafat.

Here is Clinton's description of how the negotiations at Camp David in July 2000 foundered:

> It was after midnight when Barak finally came to me with proposals. They were less than what [Shlomo] Ben-Ami and [Gilead] Sher [two members of the Israeli negotiating team] had already presented to the Palestinians. Ehud wanted me to present them to Arafat as U.S. proposals. I understood his frustration with Arafat, but I couldn't do that; it would have been a disaster, and I told him so. We talked until two-thirty. At three-fifteen he came back, and we talked another hour alone on the back porch of my cabin. Essentially he gave me the go-ahead to see if I could work out a deal on Jerusalem and the West Bank that he could live with and that was consistent with what ben-Ami and Sher had discussed with their counterparts. That was worth staying up for.
> ... [The next day], Arafat balked at not having sovereignty over all of East Jerusalem, including the Temple

Mount. He turned the offer down. I asked him to think about it. While he fretted and Barak fumed, I called Arab leaders for support. Most wouldn't say much, for fear of undercutting Arafat.

On the ninth day, I gave Arafat my best shot again. Again he said no. *Israel had gone much further than he had,* and he wouldn't even embrace their moves as the basis for future negotiations [emphasis added].[16]

Clinton tried again, in December 2000 and January 2001. In his memoirs, he devotes a page and a half to describing in detail the parameters for a settlement that he proposed to both the Palestinians and the Israelis. In Clinton's words, "I knew the plan was tough for both parties, but it was time—past time—to put up or shut up." Here is his account of what happened next:

Arafat immediately began to equivocate, asking for "clarifications." But the parameters were clear; either he would negotiate within them or not. As always, he was playing for more time. I called Mubarak and read him the points. He said they were historic and he could encourage Arafat to accept them.

On the twenty-seventh [of December], Barak's cabinet endorsed the parameters with reservations, but all their reservations were within the parameters, and therefore subject to negotiations anyway. It was historic: an Israeli government had said that to get peace, there would be a Palestinian state in roughly 97 percent of the West Bank, counting the swap, and all of Gaza, where Israel also had settlements. The ball was in Arafat's court.[17]

Days passed, with no clear response from Arafat. Clinton describes a January 2001 visit by Arafat to the White House, in which a seemingly confused Arafat continued to raise objections that seemed substanceless to Clinton. "When he left," Clinton remarks, "I still had no idea what Arafat was going to do. His body language said no, but the deal was so good I couldn't believe anyone would be foolish enough to let it go."[18]

But Arafat was. Here is how Clinton's account of the effort concludes:

> The parties continued their talks in Taba, Egypt. They got close, but they did not succeed. Arafat never said no; he just couldn't bring himself to say yes. Pride goeth before the fall. . . . Arafat's rejection of my proposal after Barak accepted it was an error of historic proportions.[19]

It's hard to believe that Carter's misleading account is supposed to be a serious attempt to describe these same events. It's clear that, in reality, the Israelis made repeated offers to Arafat that went further toward accommodating Palestinian wishes than any previous offers had ever gone—and that Arafat simply refused to accept any of these offers, not even as the basis for further negotiations. No wonder Clinton finds himself quoting and agreeing with what "Abba Eban had said long ago, the Palestinians never miss an opportunity to miss an opportunity."[20]

Look back at Carter's version. Note the disingenuousness with which Carter quotes the words of Ehud Barak in dismissing the importance of the Taba discussions. As Carter surely knows, Barak made these comments in the midst of an Israeli election campaign when his handling of the peace process was a major political issue. Barak was, of course, required by domestic political considerations to downplay his disappointment over the failure of the Taba talks and, even more important, to deny having made any major concessions that the Palestinians could try to claim later. For Carter—himself an experienced, canny politician—to cite these sentences as proof that the Israelis weren't negotiating in good faith is just silly.

What's more, Carter inadvertently reveals that he is fully aware of this fact! He affixes to Barak's comments the following footnote: "Despite this official disclaimer, substantive discussions were held at Taba, which proved to be the foundation for what evolved into the Geneva Initiative, to be described in Chapter 13." Carter is trying to have it both ways. When it suits his argument, he claims that the Taba talks were meaningless; in the next breath, he calls them "substantive" so that he can claim them as precursors of the Geneva Initiative, the subsequent peace effort with which he himself was associated.

The lapse in logic underscores Carter's desperation to line up the facts so that they support his case. But the facts don't budge.

———————◆———————

Perhaps we can agree that, at least, President Carter's version of the history of the Middle East is inadequate and, in some places, seriously misleading. But what about his policy prescriptions? Do these salvage some value for his book?

Viewed in the abstract, the political and diplomatic goals that Carter seeks are not particularly troubling. Like most decent people, he wants peace and justice in the Middle East. In pursuit of this objective, he calls for a two-state solution, with Palestinians and Israelis living securely side by side in their own countries. This, of course, is also the policy of Israel. The problem is his obsession with blaming Israel for this goal not being achieved. There are several serious problems with this approach—aside from its sheer factual inaccuracy.

First, Carter's blame-Israel stance encourages Israel-bashers around the world. The legitimizing factor of being able to quote a former president of the United States and winner of the Nobel Peace Prize when attempting to defend anti-Zionist misstatements cannot be overestimated.

Secondly, Carter's position gives comfort to the extremists on the Palestinian side who are reinforced in their extremism by this kind of "analysis." By uncritically endorsing Palestinian denunciations of Israel and blindly accepting Palestinian claims of self-justification, Carter confirms the Palestinian hardliners in their belief that Israel is an illegitimate state whose every demand must be resisted and whose very existence is improper; and in their belief that when battling such an evil enemy, every weapon—including terrorist attacks on the innocent—is justifiable.

Disturbingly, there is evidence in Carter's book that his encouragement of Palestinian extremism is not inadvertent but deliberate.

Consider this paragraph from near the end of the book, in the chapter entitled "Summary," in which Carter presents his general recommendations for the region:

> An important fact to remember is that President Mahmoud Abbas retains all presidential authority that was exercised by Yasir Arafat when he negotiated the Oslo Agreement, and the Hamas prime minister has stated that his government supports peace talks between Israel and Abbas. He added that Hamas would modify its rejection of Israel if there is a negotiated agreement that Palestinians can approve (as specified in the Camp David Accords). It is imperative that the general Arab community and all significant Palestinian groups make it clear that they will end the suicide bombings and other acts of terrorism when international laws and the ultimate goals of the Roadmap for Peace are accepted by Israel.[21]

This paragraph requires a bit of unpacking to recognize just how breathtakingly one-sided it is. Hamas, we are told, will "modify its rejection of Israel if there is a negotiated agreement that Palestinians can approve." Think about what this says. If and when a complete peace settlement acceptable to the Palestinians is achieved—apparently as judged and determined unilaterally by them—then and only then will Hamas "modify [not necessarily abandon!] its rejection of Israel." In other words, Hamas *may* someday accept Israel's right to exist, but only after the Palestinians have received everything they want at the negotiating table! Forget the commonsense idea that negotiations should *begin* with both sides acknowledging the right of the other to live in peace and freedom—such an acknowledgement, as far as the Palestinians are concerned (with Carter's support) is a *possible* end product, to be achieved only after negotiations have been concluded to the Palestinians' own satisfaction.

Here's an analogy: A tense hostage standoff is in progress. A gunman who has already used violence on others is holding a prisoner and has his gun to her head. Negotiators demand that he release the prisoner or at least lower his gun. He replies, "After you agree to give me everything I want, including a flight to freedom, I will *modify* my threat to the hostage." Does this seem like a reasonable position for the gunman to take? Is it conceivable that the police would consider this an acceptable basis for negotiations? Apparently Jimmy Carter would.

And then consider the meaning of this last sentence in that paragraph: "It is imperative that the general Arab community and all significant Palestinian groups make it clear that they will end the suicide bombings and other acts of terrorism when international laws and the ultimate goals of the Roadmap for Peace are accepted by Israel." Here, again, the concessions are all to be on one side. Carter is urging the Arabs and the Palestinians to promise that they will cease terrorism— but only *after* Israel accedes to all their demands.

As Carter makes clear throughout the book, his interpretation of "international laws" runs parallel to that of the Palestinians: If Israel wants peace, it must *first* turn over all the territory the Palestinians claim. In justification of this demand, they advance their own one-sided interpretations of various UN resolutions—specifically, UN Security Council Resolutions 194, 242, 338, and 465. As Kenneth Stein notes, Carter offers only a "partisan rendition" of these resolutions, subtly transforming them into calls for unconditional Israeli withdrawal from territories in exchange for nothing but promises of negotiations from the Palestinians.[22]

Until the most intransigent of the Palestinians get what they want, they are apparently—in Jimmy Carter's eyes—justified in continuing their acts of terrorism. Remember what he wrote: They should promise to end the suicide bombings when Israel accepts their demands—not before. The analogy to the hostage-holding gunman is complete.

As a result, to the extent that a book can affect world affairs, *Palestine: Peace Not Apartheid* is likely to have precisely the opposite effect from the one Carter claims to hope for: It will delay rather than accelerate the journey toward peace in the Middle East. In the end, it is the Palestinians themselves who are hurt by Carter's biased approach because they become even further entrenched in their illusions about weakening Israel and the need not to change. As Kenneth Stein has perceptively remarked,

> By adopting so completely the Palestinian historical narrative, Carter may hamper diplomatic efforts enshrined in the "Road Map" and elsewhere that attempt to compel the Palestinian leadership to accept accountability for its actions. In pursuing this path, Carter violates the advice he gave eighty Palestinian business, religious, and political leaders on March 16, 1983, when, speaking to a gathering at the U.S. consulate in Jerusalem, he said, "Unless you take your own destiny into your own hands and stop relying on others," you will not have a state.[23]

As disturbing as Carter's simplistic approach, his one-sided analysis, and his factual errors are, however, even more disturbing is his picking up on the Mearsheimer and Walt theme of Jewish control of American foreign policy. Referring to U.S. policy and the "condoning" of Israel's actions, Carter says:

> There are constant and vehement political and media debates in Israel concerning its policies in the West Bank but because of powerful political, economic, and religious forces in the United States, Israeli government decisions are rarely questioned or condemned, voices from Jerusalem dominate our media, and most American citizens are unaware of circumstances in the occupied territories.[24]

In other words, the old canard and conspiracy theory of Jewish control of the media, Congress, and the U.S. government is rearing its ugly head—this time, carrying all the prestige of a former president.

It is sad that Mr. Carter would attempt to use his influence in this way. It is dangerous because he will be used by elements that want to undermine support for Israel in this country. And today, with *Palestine: Peace Not Apartheid* having been ensconced on the best-seller lists, it is all too easy to imagine the anti-Semites of the world eagerly scanning its pages for quotations they can use to bolster their case with the prestige of a Nobel Peace laureate.

Perhaps Clinton's Middle East envoy Dennis Ross says it best:

> Nothing has done more to perpetuate the conflict between Arabs and Israelis than the mythologies on each side. The

mythologies about who is responsible for the conflict (and about its core issues) have taken on a life of their own. They shape perception. They allow each side to blame the other while avoiding the need to face up to its own mistakes. So long as myths are perpetuated, no one will have to face reality.[25]

It's terribly sad—and potentially tragic—that a former U.S. president should be doing so much to perpetuate myths that themselves constitute roadblocks to peace.

Of course, President Carter could not ignore the outcry his book provoked upon its publication. In an effort to stem the tide of anger, he tried meeting with groups of Jewish Americans, seeking to defend his position and defuse the controversy. After a meeting with a small group of rabbis in Phoenix, Arizona, he wrote an open letter to Jewish Americans describing the encounter:

> I emphasized, as I had throughout the tour [to promote *Palestine: Peace Not Apartheid*], that the book was about conditions and events in the Palestinian territories and not in Israel, where a democracy exists with all the freedoms we enjoy in our country and Israeli Jews and Arabs are legally guaranteed the same rights as citizens.
> We discussed the word "apartheid," which I defined as the forced segregation of two peoples living in the same land, with one of them dominating and persecuting the other. I

made clear in the book's text and in my response to the rabbis that the system of apartheid in Palestine is not based on racism but the desire of a minority of Israelis for Palestinian land and the resulting suppression of protests that involve violence. Bishop Tutu, Nelson Mandela, and prominent Israelis, including former attorney general Ben Yair, who served under both Labor and Likud prime ministers, have used and explained the appellation in harsher terms than I, pointing out that this cruel oppression is contrary to the tenets of the Jewish faith and the basic principles of the nation of Israel.

Having traveled throughout the Holy Land during the past 33 years, especially within the occupied areas, I was qualified to describe the situation from my own personal observations. In addition, The Carter Center has monitored the Palestinian elections of 1996, 2005, and 2006, which required a thorough and intimate involvement with Palestinian citizens, candidates, public officials, and also the top political leaders of Israel who controlled checkpoints throughout the West Bank and Gaza and all facets of the elections in East Jerusalem.

I made it clear that I have never claimed that American Jews control the news media, but reiterated that the overwhelming bias for Israel comes from among Christians like me who have been taught since childhood to honor and protect God's chosen people from among whom came our own savior, Jesus Christ. An additional factor, especially in the political arena, is the powerful influence of the American Israel Public Affairs Committee, which is exercising its legitimate goal of explaining the current policies of Israel's government and arousing maximum support in our country. There are no significant countervailing voices.[26]

As you can imagine, this message—with its lame and inaccurate after-the-fact reframing of the word "apartheid," its rather haughty appeal to Carter's personal experiences as justification for all the misstatements in the book, and its downright false assertion that "no significant countervailing voices" are heard in the debate over Middle East policy—fell far short of undoing the damage done by Carter's book. Together with ADL national chairman Glen S. Lewy, I wrote the ADL's own response, addressed directly to President Carter. It said, in part:

No matter the distinction you articulate in your letter, using the incendiary word "Apartheid" to refer to Israel and its policies is unacceptable and shameful. Apartheid, that abhorrent and racist system in South Africa, has no bearing on Israeli policies. Not only are Israel's policies not racist, but the situation in the territories does not arise from Israeli intentions to oppress or repress Palestinians, but is a product of Palestinian rejection of Israel and the use of terror and violence against the Jewish state. Nothing illustrates the stark difference better than Israel's offer of withdrawal made at Camp David and its unilateral withdrawal from Gaza.

Your efforts in the letter to minimize the impact of your charge that American Jews control U.S. Middle East policy are simply unconvincing. In both your book and in your many television and print interviews you have been feeding into conspiracy theories about excessive Jewish power and control. Considering the history of anti-Semitism, even in our great country, this is very dangerous stuff.

To belatedly claim that you were really talking all along about Christian support for Israel, which you disrespectfully call "bias," neither repairs the damage of your accusations nor eases our concerns. Millions of American Christians support Israel because of their deeply felt religious beliefs and because they understand that Israel is a democracy, an ally of America, and on the front line to combat terror.

We continue to be distressed about the role you have taken upon yourself with regard to Israel and American Jews. Indeed, we know that the rabbis with whom you met in Phoenix are similarly distressed.

True sensitivity to Israel and American Jews would be demonstrated by ceasing these one-sided attacks and apologizing for damaging the good name of the State of Israel and the Jewish people.[27]

It's tempting to speculate as to why President Carter has developed his appalling blind spot about the State of Israel and his consequent sharp tilt toward the Palestinians. He is a man whose personal and public lives have been deeply intertwined. People in America and around the world have come to know a lot about his background, his values, and his private life: his boyhood in Depression-era Georgia, his traditional Christian upbringing, his service in the U.S. Navy, his colorful family (feisty Miss Lillian, eccentric brother Billy), his well-documented opposition to racial segregation.

It seems likely that Carter's religious views have colored his response to the peoples of the Middle East. Unlike the majority of Southern Baptists who now see the creation and strength of the State of Israel as part of the divine plan, he maintains a more traditional view that focuses on Jewish sin. Listen to what he says about his first visit to Israel in the early 1970s: "It was especially interesting to visit with some of the surviving Samaritans, who complained to us that their holy sites and culture were not being respected by Israeli authorities—the same complaint heard by Jesus and his disciples almost two thousand years earlier."[28]

As Jeffrey Goldberg wrote in his review of Carter's book, "One gets the impression that Carter believes that Israelis—in their deviousness—somehow mean to keep Jesus from fulfilling the demands of His ministry."[29]

Another indicator of Carter's thinking appears in a revealing passage early in *Palestine: Peace Not Apartheid.* Carter further describes his first visit to Israel in 1973 in these words:

> I have to admit that, at the time, I equated the ejection of Palestinians from their previous homes within the State of Israel to the forcing of Lower Creek Indians from the Georgia land where our family farm was now located; they had been moved west to Oklahoma on the "Trail of Tears" to make room for our white ancestors.[30]

Carter hedges this observation in a curious way. He introduces it with the clause, "I have to admit," as though he finds it somehow embarrassing to confess these feelings about the Palestinians. And he specifies that this is how he viewed their situation "at the time," although nowhere in the book does he explain when, how, or why his attitude might have changed. I must say that I don't understand what this hedging is all about. But I think it suggests that the topic is emotionally charged for President Carter.

And perhaps we can understand why. The comparison of the Palestinians to the Native Americans who were driven from the land to make room for the Carters' own family farm implies that President Carter feels an uncomfortable sense of *identification* with the Jews of Israel. Perhaps Carter—strict, self-judging Baptist that he is—feels some degree of shame over the land seizure that provided a historic basis for his own family's wealth. That would be understandable; the "Trail of Tears" episode of 1838, which resulted in the deaths of an estimated four thousand Cherokee men, women, and children, is considered one of the most disgraceful acts in the long, sad story of American mistreatment of the Indians.

If the flight of the Palestinians at the time of the founding of Israel reminds Carter of the unhappy fate of the original inhabitants of his own ancestral lands, perhaps he now is projecting onto the Jews of Israel his own sense of inherited guilt. In an odd way, Carter's harsh treatment of Israel in *Palestine: Peace Not Apartheid* may be an unconscious attempt to expiate his own guilt over the mistreatment of the Indians nearly two centuries ago. His sensitivity to the plight of the dispossessed may be admirable, but not when it leads him to adopt and disseminate an inaccurate and misleading version of history.

Can I prove that this theory is correct? Of course not. I'm sure President Carter would disavow any such connection between the two historical episodes and his own posture regarding the Middle East. But it seems to me that some explanation is required for why this conscientious statesman and spokesman for peace should have developed such a one-sided and unfair position on a conflict filled with so many complexities and such admittedly tragic consequences. Perhaps this explanation is as good as any.

Our discussion has come full circle. Jimmy Carter, as I have said, is in many ways a good man. Which makes it all the more tragic that he has written a book about one of today's most significant global conflicts that is filled with distortions, misstatements, misunderstandings, and errors—a book whose primary effect will be to give comfort and support to bigots and opportunists whose chief goal is the destruction of a nation and its people.

6

THE WAY
FORWARD

A S AMERICA PONDERS THE CHALLENGES IT FACES IN OUR troubled world, it is crucial that we think clearly and honestly about the choices ahead.

We're all tempted to retreat to comfortable verities and black-and-white visions of the world—especially if those visions seem to offer hope of escaping from the sobering responsibilities and daunting difficulties that seem to be America's lot. Once again, for those who seek a respite from these challenges, it is terribly tempting to blame the Jews.

Instead, I'd suggest that a dose of realistic thinking based on facts, not fantasies, is the better prescription for our country—and for the world.

As I write, one of our greatest challenges is what to do in Iraq. In that unhappy country, a war launched by the United States and its allies based on assumptions that were widely accepted but that have proved to be largely mistaken has been seriously mismanaged. One terrible situation—a powerful, strategically central Middle Eastern nation in the grip of a ruthless despot with a known proclivity for threatening his neighbors—has been exchanged for another—a country in the grip of sectarian violence, teetering on the brink of civil war, struggling to find a future as either a united collection of diverse ethnic and religious groups or as a loose federation of largely independent states. The danger is that once the inevitable pull-out of American forces occurs, Iraq will devolve into a failed state, a potential new stronghold for Islamist extremists and terrorist groups.

Americans and, indeed, the rest of the world are engaged in a vigorous debate as to what we should do now about this painful situation. As everyone realizes, the choices ahead have enormous implications for the rest of the Middle East. The debate is important and vitally necessary.

Part of that debate is a post-mortem on the Bush administration's leadership. How and where did we go wrong? What lessons must we learn from the errors in Iraq? What principles for sound decision making should we take away from the mistakes of the 2003–2007 period?

Again, this kind of analysis is necessary and important. Yet, here is one area in which the temptation to blame the Jews is ever-present. When a great and good nation makes mistakes, it is nice to believe that "we Americans" really weren't to blame. Maybe we can find someone else to blame—an alien group that, somehow, misled or deceived us, dragging us against our better judgment into a war that we should never have fought.

As we've seen, some of those engaged in the debate about the Middle East have yielded to this temptation. They've chosen to blame the so-called neocons for America's mistakes in Iraq. And some have gone further, painting a picture of these sinister neocons as mostly Jews and (horrors!) staunch supporters of Israel. The implications: The war in Iraq was never about any of the things the Bush administration and its supporters claimed—never about the tyranny of Saddam Hussein, the threat of weapons of mass destruction, the danger of regimes that support terrorism, or the need to strengthen democracy in the Middle East—it was always about a secret, unstated objective: to make the region safer for Israel.

It would be tragic if this belief came to dominate the historical record on Iraq. And it would be worse if it distorted the debate about where we go from here. As we've seen, the U.S. government made its decisions about war in Iraq, for good or ill, based on its perceptions of American interests in the region and in the world. That's the right basis for its future decisions affecting Iraq. Americans debating what our country should do next need to remain focused on these realities—not get sidetracked into a fantasy argument about Israel's supposed role in fomenting war.

The same applies to the burgeoning debate about another great power in the region that is potentially threatening to peace and to American interests: Iran.

Everyone knows why Iran has moved to the forefront of world anxieties about the Middle East. It's a large, populous nation in the very center of the region. It controls a large fraction of the world's oil reserves. It is heavily armed, with one of the world's largest military forces. It is ruled by a reactionary Islamist regime that oppresses its own people, stifles dissent, and has openly threatened its neighbors (including Israel). And in the last three years it has moved toward creating nuclear weapons in defiance of international treaties and the expressed will of the United Nations. Clearly Iran is a big and growing problem on the world stage, and the one remaining superpower, the United States, has an obligation to lead the nations in dealing with that problem.

As one might expect, there are voices within the United States arguing on every conceivable side. Some are demanding aggressive action by America, from preventive bombing of Iran's nuclear sites to outright invasion of the country. Others emphasize the need for diplomatic engagement supplemented by economic pressure through international sanctions. Still others advocate a middle ground, calling for tough negotiations supported by a credible threat of military action. Chastened by the experience in Iraq, most Americans are hoping to avoid a new war in the region. But most appear to be concerned enough about the Iranian threat to agree that, in the parlance of the day, "no option should be off the table"—including the possibility of military action.

Again, this is a vitally important debate that must be pursued vigorously. And that means not allowing discussion to be sidetracked by phony issues. Of course, I believe that the security of Israel is one important element in any debate about the future of the Middle East. The vast majority of Americans feel the same way. There's no reason we should have to squander time and attention in a metadebate over whether the status of Israel has played too important a role in the development of policy toward Iran.

Unfortunately, some voices in the policy arena are eager to engage in just such a metadebate. As we've noted, Mearsheimer and Walt devoted several pages in their article to warning against the supposed plans of the Israel Lobby to embroil the United States in a needless war in Iran. Or consider Scott Ritter, the former arms inspector who has made a reputation as an opinionated, somewhat volatile advocate of a changing array of positions on Middle Eastern policy. In his recent book *Target Iran*, Ritter warns against the danger of a new U.S.-led war against Iran. That's a legitimate policy position, of course. But then Ritter goes out of his way to blame the Jews, implying that pro-Israel lobbyists in the U.S. are responsible for exaggerating the perception of the Iranian threat:

> The conflict currently underway between the United States and Iran is, first and foremost, a conflict born in Israel. It is

based upon an Israeli contention that Iran poses a threat to Israel, and defined by Israeli assertions that Iran possesses a nuclear weapons program. None of this has been shown to be
true, and indeed much of the allegations made by Israel
against Iran have been clearly demonstrated as being false.
And yet the United States continues to trumpet the Israeli
claims. . . .

Israel has, through a combination of ignorance, fear, and
paranoia, elevated Iran to a threat status that it finds unacceptable. Israel has engaged in policies that have further in-
flamed this situation. Israel displays an arrogance and rigidity
when it comes to developing any diplomatic solution to the
Iranian issue. And Israel demands that the United States take
the lead in holding Iran to account. Israel threatens military
action against Iran, knowing only too well that in doing so Israel would be committing America to war as well. When it
comes to Iran, Israel can no longer be said to be behaving as a
friend of America. And it is high time we in America had the
courage to recognize this, and take appropriate actions.[1]

If the U.S. *does* invade Iran, Ritter suggests, it will be, like Iraq,
another disaster produced by the neocons and other supporters of
Israel—the fault of the Jews, in short. Ritter goes so far as to play the
"treason" card, leveling the old accusation of dual loyalty against
American Jews:

It is fine to be sympathetic and supportive of the state of Israel. I know I am. But it is never acceptable as an American to
subordinate the national interest of your homeland for the
sake and benefit of another nation. In the past, such behavior

has been likened to sedition and treason. And just because the action is undertaken on behalf of Israel does not make it any less so than if it had been done on behalf of any other nation.[2]

Does Ritter explicitly say that American Jews who advocate a tough stance in regard to Iran's nuclear ambitions are guilty of treason against the United States? Not quite . . . not in so many words. Perhaps he (or his editor) realizes that to say this explicitly would expose how exaggerated and absurd the notion is. But, he skirts such an accusation and thereby helps revive and sustain the age-old canard that Jews are treacherous, disloyal, not to be trusted.

What's the proper U.S. stance toward Iran? Under what circumstances should we consider military action against that country? Do you want to contend that the United States should keep its hands off Iran, even if that country does develop nuclear weapons? Fine—make your case, and may the best argument carry the day. There's more than one legitimate position to be taken on these issues. And there's room for discussion and debate over how the American alliance with Israel should impact our thinking. But there's *no* room for the Ritteresque strategy of blaming the Jews.

Here is another way in which bigotry about Israel and the Jews distorts the important debate about American foreign policy in the Middle East. Most people agree that a lasting peace in the region will ultimately require a comprehensive settlement of major issues involving all the interested parties. Resolving any single conflict may be important. But in the long run, true peace will require justice and security for all the peoples of the region. And that means that, ultimately, settlement of the so-called Arab-Israeli conflict is a necessary building block.

All of this is accepted by most people of good will, including most Israelis and American supporters of Israel. It means that the United States can't afford to neglect the Arab-Israeli issue and focus strictly on other regional matters such as Iraq or Iran. As long as conflict continues to simmer between Israel and its neighbors—as long as suicide bomb missions and missile attacks continue to strike Israel and its people, forcing tough security measures, acts of self-defense, and sometimes counterattacks by Israel—and as long as political leaders continue to stoke hatred of Israel and the Jews as both a central tenet of their international policy and as a convenient way to deflect attention from their own failings as domestic leaders—as long as these inherently destabilizing conditions continue to exist, there is always the danger that hostilities involving Israel may again escalate into open warfare and perhaps threaten a larger regional war. So somehow, some way, in the long run, a path to peace, security, and mutual acceptance between Israel and its neighbors *must* be found if peace is to rule in the Middle East.

This simple truism, however, has been subtly distorted by some people with a not-so-innocent agenda. And their formulation of the situation has been allowed by others to distort the world's priorities when considering the future of the region.

The distorted version of the simple reality I described above is usually stated something like this: "The conflict between Israel and the

Palestinians is the central issue in the Middle East. It is at the heart of all other disputes involving the Arab and Islamic worlds, and until it is settled there can be no peace in the region."

Notice how the nature of the issue is subtly shifted in the formulation I just cited.

First, the conflict over Israel is described as "Israel versus the Palestinians." This is, in itself, a tendentious and distorted way to think about the problems in the Middle East.

The rights, interests, and needs of the Palestinian people are certainly important and a legitimate cause for concern. Like all other peoples, the Palestinians deserve the opportunity to live in peace, to own their own lands, and to pursue happiness in the way they choose, provided they respect the rights of their neighbors to enjoy the same privileges. The so-called two-state solution, which has been accepted in theory and practice by all the concerned parties, is the agreed-upon path to ensuring that both the Palestinians and the Israelis will enjoy those rights.

The difficulty, of course, lies in how we reach the two-state solution. Like the Palestinians, the Israelis want a stable and secure nation within defensible borders. Drawing those borders and ensuring that Israel and its people will be safe behind them has proven to be a difficult matter. The fact that Israel continues to be the target of military and terrorist attacks from its neighbors, including both the Palestinians and their allies in Lebanon and elsewhere, puts Israeli leaders in a seemingly impossible situation. How can they work out and enforce a fair settlement with an enemy that continues to attack them, denies their legitimacy, and refuses to renounce the ultimate objective of destroying them?

The problem, of course, is much bigger than Israel and the Palestinians. The problem is that Israel is bordered not just by the Palestinian territories but by an array of hostile Arab states that have mostly refused to play a positive role in resolving the tensions in the region. In fact, they have exacerbated those tensions largely because it serves their domestic purposes to have Israel and the Jews as handy scapegoats for all the problems of the region.

This is one of the reasons that the other Arab states, such as Jordan, flatly refused for decades to resettle or otherwise assist the Palestinian people. It served the purposes of the Arab leaders to be able to point to the aggrieved Palestinians as victims of big, bad Israel. The grievances of the Palestinians became a convenient excuse for the unrelenting hostility of the Arab states, as well as for the economic and political failures of those same Arab states.

For these reasons, describing the issue as one of "Israel and the Palestinians" serves the purposes of pro-Arab and anti-Israel propaganda. It throws the spotlight on the problems and rights of the Palestinian people, creating the implication that it is up to Israel to redress those problems and ensure those rights. At the same time, it throws a shadow over the bigger issue of "Israel and the Arab states," obscuring the fact that most of the countries in the region still refuse to recognize Israel, to guarantee its freedom and security, and to promise not to attack Israel or to support terrorists who launch such attacks. This formulation transforms Israel—a tiny country surrounded by hostile neighbors—into the "big bully" picking on the helpless Palestinians, and provides all the other powers in the region with a handy excuse for doing nothing to promote a *real* peace agreement in the Middle East.

Furthermore, naming the Israeli-Palestinian conflict as the central issue in the Middle East distorts the discussion of the future of the Middle East by apparently justifying any degree of Arab or Islamist intransigence, hatred, and violence directed toward either Israel or the United States.

As we've seen, the idea that the global Islamist movement is mainly driven by resentment over Israel's treatment of the Palestinians is a canard. But it's a useful one for propaganda purposes.

The fact that Israel exercises a degree of control over the lives and movements of Palestinian people in the territories under its jurisdiction is an uncomfortable reality for the Israeli people. The Jews created Israel not in order to have dominion over any other people but simply in order to have a homeland they could call their own and in which they could live in peace, ruling themselves as they saw fit. In self-defense, the Israelis were forced to take control of some Palestinian lands, which to this day are a source of attacks against Israel. Against its will, Israel was put in the position of being a conqueror. It's an unnatural state for the Israelis, whose faith in democracy, freedom, and self-determination is deeply rooted. They want to get out of the position of governing the Palestinians as quickly as possible—as long as the price is not national suicide.

Israelis, then, are deeply ambivalent about the Palestinian territories. Some might say they have a guilt complex about them. Almost every other country in history has, at some point, taken lands from its neighbors, sometimes for reasons that can be justified, sometimes not. To pick an obvious example, every square inch of the United States was taken from its previous owners at some point, often by force of arms. But because of Israel's humanistic heritage, its idealistic origins, and the religious and ethical traditions of its people, Israel agonizes over the territories it holds far more than other nations do.

This is what makes "the Palestinian issue" such a tempting propaganda tool for Israel's enemies. The Palestinian territories are the one potential moral weak spot in the case for Israel. Everyone, including the Israelis, agrees that the Palestinians should govern themselves, though bringing this about has proven to be painfully difficult. But as long as some Palestinians remain under Israeli rule, this fact can be pointed to by the Arab regimes and their sympathizers around the world as "proof" that Israel is power-hungry, tyrannical, racist, an obstacle to peace and freedom.

It's the one argument the Islamists have in their bill of grievances against the West that gives a semiplausible moral strength to their position. This is why they harp on it whenever they get the chance. And this is why it is important for clear-headed thinkers to reject the formulation that describes the Palestinian-Israeli conflict as "the key to peace in the Middle East." Yes, it's vitally important that the Palestinian people have a homeland of their own, governed democratically and with integrity, in which they can live in peace with their neighbors. But this is just one of several equally important keys to long-term peace in the Middle East. The other keys include a genuine commitment to democracy by the autocratic regimes of the region; a renunciation of the quest for territorial expansion by countries in the Middle East; a disavowal of sectarian violence; and, yes, recognition of Israel's right to exist within secure, defensible borders.

To say that the rights of the Palestinians trump all these other concerns—and to imply that, until the Palestinians get their rights, none of these other issues can be addressed—is absurd, hypocritical, and a barrier to peace.

In the vital struggle to find a path to peace, the debate over Jewish control of U.S. foreign policy ignited by Mearsheimer and Walt is playing a damaging role. Within the West, it serves to distract policymakers and the general public from the substantive issues that must be addressed—Iraq, Iran, a Palestinian settlement, and so on. In the Arab countries, the influence of the Israel Lobby controversy may be more pernicious.

In April 2007, the well-known *New York Times* columnist David Brooks attended a conference in Jordan that was cosponsored by the Center for Strategic Studies at the University of Jordan and the American Enterprise Institute. I want to quote Brooks's account of what happened at the conference at some length because I find it both significant and disturbing. The goal of the conference, Brooks explains, was to bring together moderate Arab reformers with American experts and leaders to discuss ways of moving toward peace and democracy in the Middle East. He writes:

As it happened, though, the Arab speakers mainly wanted to talk about the Israel lobby. One described a book edited in the mid-1990s by the Jewish policy analyst David Wurmser [a reference to *Tyranny's Ally: America's Failure to Defeat Saddam Hussein*] as the secret blueprint for American foreign policy over the past decade. A pollster showed that large majorities in Arab countries believe that the Israel lobby has more influence over American policy than the Bush administration. Speaker after speaker triumphantly cited the work of Stephen Walt, John Mearsheimer and Jimmy Carter as proof that even Americans were coming to admit that the Israel lobby controls their government.

The problems between America and the Arab world have nothing to do with religious fundamentalism or ideological extremism, several Arab speakers argued. They have to do with American policies toward Israel, and the forces controlling those policies.

... But the striking thing about this meeting was the emotional tone. There seemed to be a time, after 9/11, when it was generally accepted that terror and extremism were symptoms of a deeper Arab malaise. There seemed to be a general recognition that the Arab world had fallen behind, and that it needed economic, political and religious modernization.

But there was nothing defensive or introspective about the Arab speakers here. In response to Bernard Lewis's question, "What Went Wrong?" their answer seemed to be: Nothing's wrong with us. What's wrong with you?

The events of the past three years have shifted their diagnosis of where the cancer is—from dysfunction in the Arab world to malevolence in Jerusalem and in Aipac [*sic*]. Furthermore, the Walt and Mearsheimer paper on the Israel lobby has had a profound effect on Arab elites. It has encouraged them not to be introspective, not to think about their own problems, but to blame everything on the villainous Israeli network.[3]

Again, we run into the problem of guilt by association. It would be unfair to hold the loosely allied group of pundits that includes Mearsheimer, Walt, Carter, and Tony Judt strictly responsible for how their ideas are used—or misused—in the Arab world. It's a point on which Judt, in particular, leans heavily, often quoting some words attributed to the anti-Communist writer Arthur Koestler: "You cannot help it if idiots and bigots share your views for their reasons. That doesn't mean you can be tarred with their views."[4]

And this is right—up to a point. None of us can be held accountable for every use of our words or ideas by other people over whom we have no control. But when you find your views being quoted gleefully by people whose perspectives and goals all decent people find repugnant (as avowed racist David Duke has been gleefully quoting Mearsheimer and Walt); when your authority is invoked in support of extreme, exaggerated, and outlandish distortions of reality (e.g., "the Israel lobby has more influence over American policy than the Bush administration"!); and when your writings are cited to justify intransigence, delay, and scapegoating that are virtually guaranteed to throw up roadblocks on the path to peace—when this is the way your words are being used in the world, is it really morally justifiable to disavow *any* responsibility?

Those in the blame-the-Lobby crowd have put themselves in the position of the arms peddler who sells cheap handguns out of the back of his car on the streets of tough neighborhoods, then expresses shock and surprise when crooks and gangsters use those weapons to stick up stores and mug old ladies.

At the very least, when people such as Mearsheimer, Walt, Judt, and Carter discover that their writings are being used to foster hatred, bigotry, and intransigence, they ought to take the initiative to publicly protest such use, denounce its perpetrators, and distance themselves from such interpretations of their work. And they should take steps to ensure that their protests are publicized and disseminated at least as widely as their original writings and the even-more-extreme interpretations founded on those writings by enemies of peace. One would think that they would be eager to do this—if not out of simple human decency, at least in the interests of protecting their own reputations. But too often, they lapse into silence, or fall back on the lame "I'm-not-responsible" excuse.

Also note: I don't mean to suggest that responsibility for the problems of the Middle East lies all on one side. I agree with David Brooks that the leaders of the Arab world would be well advised to exercise a bit of introspection. The dysfunctions of the countries they call home are well known: the widespread poverty and underdevelopment that persists even in countries with vast oil reserves; the absence of democratic political processes, including truly free elections, an unfettered press, and open debate; the repression of women; the rampant self-dealing and corruption on the part of government officials; the official encouragement of racism and anti-Semitism in the media, in schools, and in the mosques. All of these are major obstacles to prosperity and modernization in the region as well as roadblocks on the path to peace. Positive change in the Arab world would be a welcome step forward that the peoples of both Israel and the United States would hail.

Nor am I disavowing any Israeli role in the peace process, nor declaring that Israel can or should sit back passively until thorough reform sweeps through the Arab lands. Nearly all Israeli leaders—like the people of Israel—are willing to meet the Palestinians and all of the Arabs halfway, provided a sincere commitment to peaceful coexistence exists on their side. The past actions of the Israelis have shown their readiness to compromise. Now they are looking for the same readiness from their counterparts across the bargaining table.

It may be that in the world as seen by Mearsheimer, Walt, Judt, and Carter, all the movement, all the concessions are expected to be on the Israeli side. The Israeli response should not be equivalently rigid. Instead, I hope and trust that the people of Israel will act as they have often done in the past, setting an example for openness and generosity in the belief that, eventually, they will receive the same in return.

Our enemy, always, is simplistic thinking, rigid ideology, and the biased refusal to face facts honestly and forthrightly. When these are the dominating features of discourse on *any* side in the long struggle for peace, hatred and violence are the beneficiaries.

Those who identify themselves as "liberals" or "progressives" will have an important role to play in the ongoing quest for peace.

I've already discussed the widespread perception, which anti-Israel commentators such as Mearsheimer, Walt, Judt, and Carter play upon, that the major Jewish organizations in the United States have been captured by the "hard right" and that they promote a rigidly hawkish agenda regarding Israel, the Palestinians, and the Middle East in general. Those who subscribe to this belief use it as an excuse for labeling Israel a "threat to peace" and sometimes as "the world's greatest threat to peace"—as if a democratic state that has never sought hegemony over its neighbors could somehow compare with other regimes that have track records of threatening, undermining, and invading nearby countries.

As I've explained, I think the perception that support for Israel now amounts to a "right-wing" position is a gross oversimplification and quite unfair. The truth is that the vast majority of American Jews—like Jews everywhere in the world—are supportive of Israel, believe in the importance of a Jewish state, and recognize the right of Israel to defend itself against sworn enemies. This includes people from across the political spectrum—conservatives, moderates, liberals, and radicals—as well as millions of people who rarely think about politics but have a visceral sense of connection to Israel and their fellow Jews.

As a result, Jews who consider themselves Zionists are far from monolithic. They hold views of every conceivable stripe on almost every issue related to Israel and the Middle East. What concessions—if any—should Israel be prepared to offer in exchange for peace? If a

Palestinian state is created, how should its borders be defined? What limits—if any—should there be on Palestinian sovereignty? Is it legitimate for Israel to negotiate with leaders who refuse to abandon terrorism? Are the Israeli settlements in the territories an obstacle to peace, and, if so, what should be done with them? How should Israel deal with the changing demographics of Palestine and their implications for the future of the Jewish State? Can Israel coexist peacefully with an Islamist Iran? The questions go on and on, and you'll find smart, articulate, committed Jews on all sides of every one—which is right and proper because freewheeling debate offers the best opportunity for truth and wisdom to emerge.

Harsh critics of Israel and of American Jewry such as Mearsheimer, Walt, and Carter also recognize and appreciate the fact that Jews are not monolithic in their views. They often allude to the uninhibited nature of the debates they witness in Israel itself, and they bemoan the fact that (in their view) such open exchange is rarely seen in the United States. I've already quoted Jimmy Carter's words in which he contrasts the "constant and vehement political and media debates in Israel concerning its policies in the West Bank" and what he considers the repressive silence regarding the same issues in America.[5] In a similar vein, Tony Judt has written: "How are we to explain the fact that it is in Israel itself that the uncomfortable issues raised by Professors Mearsheimer and Walt have been most thoroughly aired?"[6] Like Carter, Judt admires the openness he sees in Israel—and uses it as a rhetorical club with which to lambaste the conformity and thought-control that are supposedly prevalent in the United States.

I've already made an effort to debunk the claims that Jewish (or indeed non-Jewish) freedom of opinion in the United States is repressed or discouraged. But I'd like to point out a couple of basic facts about the relationship between American Jewry and our counterparts in Israel that might help to explain the difference in tone—if there is one—between the debates over the Middle East that one observes in Israel and those that occur in the United States.

First, there is the reluctance to "wash one's dirty laundry in public." As the Jewish homeland, Israel is a country where Jews can freely and openly debate their future precisely because the conversation is taking place among family members, in the relative privacy of their home. Every Jew living in Israel is *by definition* committed to the freedom and security of the nation. (To feel otherwise would be to invite physical attacks *on oneself*, which is something that even a "self-hating Jew" isn't likely to do!) Therefore, people can argue vociferously about the right way to achieve that freedom and security without needing to wonder about the motivation, good faith, or personal investment of their interlocutors. Every argument is an argument among family members, which means that all the participants can assume a degree of mutual support that simply doesn't exist in any other setting.

Furthermore, the fact that a debate is occurring inside Israel, where those who participate and listen are mostly one's fellow Jews and fellow Zionists, undoubtedly encourages a more freewheeling tone. Imagine having a heated family argument across the dinner table at home about some contentious issue—the details of a daughter's wedding, for example, or what to do with a house that you've all just inherited jointly. Think about the language that might fly once the discussion *really* gets going! And now imagine the same conversation taking place, not at home but in some public place—a restaurant, say, or a local park—with strangers looking on and eavesdropping. Wouldn't you be a lot more restrained, a lot more careful about what you say, a lot more cautious about exposing your differences to public scrutiny?

A little of that same feeling of caution inevitably affects debates among Jews here in the United States. We can't help but know that others may be listening. Is there a tendency, as a result, to soft-pedal our disagreements? I suspect there is. It's a subtlety that an "outsider" like Jimmy Carter might never consider, but which helps to explain the difference in tone that Carter finds so distressing.

And here is a second factor. As an American Jew who has frequently visited Israel but who makes his home in the United States, I am acutely aware that it is my Israeli brothers and sisters who are literally on the front lines in the Middle East conflict—not I. Decisions affecting the security of Israel, its borders with the surrounding countries, the freedom of Palestinians to come and go, defenses against the threat of terrorism—all of these may have life-and-death consequences for the Jews of Jerusalem, of Tel Aviv, of Nazareth, of Haifa. By contrast, the Jews of New York, of Chicago, of San Francisco, of Atlanta face little personal danger. The very lives of the Jews of Israel are at stake in the debates—not ours.

For that reason, most Jews in America and around the world feel it's appropriate to defer to our friends and family in Israel when it comes to making crucial decisions about the future of that nation. It would be easy for us to call on Israel to make concessions for peace, to knock down security barriers, to turn over land to the Palestinians—easy to do, and a cost-free way for us to feel brave, generous, and progressive. But then the people of Israel would be the ones who would have to live with the results. Would that be fair? Would it be responsible? I don't think so.

Most American Jews leave the big decisions about war, peace, and the path to the future to the people of Israel. And most make a point of supporting the Israeli government no matter which way it may happen to lean at a given time. When the government is more conciliatory, we back it and try to promote American policies that will help the conciliatory moves to advance the cause of peace. When the government is more defensive, we back it and call for American help with those defensive efforts. Only in extreme cases, when we think our friends in Israel are making a big mistake, do we presume to criticize from our safe perches in America. (I mentioned a few such instances earlier in this book.) It's the philosophy that has always guided the Anti-Defamation League and the one to which most major Jewish American organizations subscribe.

So there are good reasons why American Jews tend to close ranks in defense of Israel, especially in terms of public debate. I think this is a natural and thoroughly appropriate way to behave. But having said this, I want to return to the role of the Jewish liberal or progressive—the person who may feel that he or she has not been fully represented in recent discussions over the future of Israel and the Middle East.

I've stressed that Jewish opinion is not monolithic, neither in Israel nor in the rest of the world. Now I want to emphasize that this is a *good* thing, a strength for our community—not a weakness. I would call on American Jews who disagree with the policies of either the Israeli government or such lobbying groups as AIPAC to be forthright and vocal in their opinions. If you believe your voices haven't been heard, speak up! Join the debate. Propose your best solutions to the thorny issues of the day—the Palestinian question, the threat of Iran, and all the rest. Don't give in to the negative voices of the Mearsheimers and other hostile critics, who describe vigorous disagreements among members of the Jewish community as "attempts to censor" or "control" the discussion. Refuse to be censored or controlled! That's the American way—and, I would submit, it's also the Jewish way.

Finally, I would urge that all people who truly care about world peace and want to help find a just solution to the problems of the Middle East should agree on certain minimal ground rules for future debate and discussion. Like almost everyone who has participated in dialogues about that troubled part of the world, I've been dismayed by the rapidity with which most conversations seem to degenerate into dual monologues in which each side talks past the other and no real listening or understanding occurs.

Let's agree to adhere to a single standard of expectations for moral behavior by all parties, rather than applying to our opponents a far stricter set of principles than we ourselves would agree to follow. Let's stipulate that deaths to civilians on *all* sides of any dispute are tragic and deplorable; that *all* people should be entitled to basic rights of freedom and decent living conditions; and that *all* nations deserve a chance to live in peace and security, without fearing violence from their neighbors.

If future conversations about the Middle East can begin with these premises, perhaps we'll have a better chance of finding common ground on which we can live together—a goal that, I like to think, all peoples of every religion and political persuasion can agree on.

NOTES

CHAPTER 1

1. Michael Oren, address before the AIPAC Policy Conference 2007, delivered March 11, 2007.
2. "ADL Survey: Anti-Semitism Declines Slightly in America; 14 Percent of Americans Hold 'Strong' Anti-Semitic Beliefs," press release, April 4, 2005, http://www.adl.org/PresRele/ASUS_12/ 4680_12.htm.
3. Charles Lindbergh, "Des Moines Speech," delivered in Des Moines, Iowa, on September 11, 1941. This speech was met with outrage in many quarters. *Charles Lindbergh: An American Aviator* Web site, http://www.charleslindbergh.com/americafirst/speech.asp.
4. Walter Laqueur, *The Changing Face of Antisemitism: From Ancient Times to the Present Day* (New York: Oxford University Press, 2006), p. 143.

5. Laurel Leff, "How the NYT Missed the Story of the Holocaust While It Was Happening," George Mason University's History News Network Web site, http://hnn.us/articles/10903.html.

6. Pat Buchanan, interview, *Talk of the Nation,* National Public Radio, May 30, 2005.

7. Quoted in Edward Shapiro, "Pat Buchanan and the Jews," *Judaism,* Spring 1996.

CHAPTER 2

1. John J. Mearsheimer and Stephen Walt, "The Israel Lobby and U.S. Foreign Policy," working paper no. RWP06–011, March 13, 2006, p. 1, *Faculty Research Working Paper Series,* John F. Kennedy School of Government Web site, http://ksgnotes1. harvard.edu/Research/wpaper.nsf/rwp/RWP06–011. Also published in a slightly condensed form as John Mearsheimer and Stephen Walt, "The Israel Lobby," *London Review of Books,* March 23, 2006, http://www.lrb.co.uk/v28/n06/print/mear01_. html. All references to the Mearsheimer and Walt paper in this book are to the version on the Kennedy School Web site.

2. Michael Massing, "The Storm over the Israel Lobby," *New York Review of Books,* June 8, 2006, http://www.nybooks.com/articles/19062.

3. Mearsheimer and Walt, "The Israel Lobby," p.10.

4. Efrain Karsh, "Falsifying the Record: Benny Morris, David Ben-Gurion, and the 'Transfer' Idea," *Israel Affairs,* Winter 1997, p. 52, cited in Alan Dershowitz, "Debunking the Newest—and Oldest—Jewish Conspiracy: A Reply to the Mearsheimer-Walt 'Working Paper,'" Harvard Law School, April 2006, http://www. ksg.harvard.edu/research/working_papers/dershowitzreply.pdf.

5. Mearsheimer and Walt, "The Israel Lobby," p.11.

6. Quoted in letter from Jeremy Schreiber, "The Israel Lobby," *London Review of Books,* April 20, 2006, http://www.lrb.co.uk/v28/n08/letters.html.

7. Benny Morris, "And Now for Some Facts," *New Republic,* May 8, 2006, cited by Meryl Yourish, http://www.yourish.com/2006/04/28/1158.

8. Mearsheimer and Walt, "The Israel Lobby," p. 11.

9. Ibid., p. 13.

10. Ibid., p. 5.

11. Mahathir Mohamad's full speech reprinted in the *Sydney Morning Herald,* Oct. 22, 2003, http://www.smh.com.au/articles/2003/10/20/1066502121884.html.

12. "Islamic Extremism: Common Concern for Muslim and Western Publics," on Pew Global Attitudes Project Web site, July 14, 2005, http://pewglobal.org/reports/display.php?ReportID=248.

13. Sharmeen Obaid Chinoy, "Pakistan: In the Land of Conspiracy Theories," *PBS Frontline/World* Web site, Aug. 24, 2005, http://www.pbs.org/frontlineworld/blog/2005/08/pakistan_in_the.html.

14. "Eight Arrested in Paris for Deadly Tunisian Synagogue Bombing," *CBC News,* Nov. 5, 2002, http://www.cbc.ca/news/story/2002/11/05/france_arrests021105.html.

15. Martin Kramer, "The American Interest: A Realist Case for the U.S.-Israel Alliance," *Wall Street Journal,* Nov. 21, 2006, http://www.opinionhournal.com/forms/printThis.html?id=110009278.

16. Mearsheimer and Walt, "The Israel Lobby," p. 15.

17. Ibid.

18. Ibid., pp. 17–18.

19. E. R. Shipp, "Chicago Politicians' New Dispute: Taking Credit for a Victory," *New York Times,* Nov. 24, 1984, http://select.nytimes.com/search/restricted/article?res=F40A16FB3D5C0C778EDDA80994DC484D81.

20. Massing, "The Storm over the Israel Lobby."

21. Quoted in J. J. Goldberg, *Jewish Power: Inside the American Jewish Establishment* (Reading, Mass.: Addison-Wesley, 1996), p. 284.

22. Mearsheimer and Walt, "The Israel Lobby," pp. 20–21.

23. See Ed Lasky, "The New York Times and the Jews," Nov. 15, 2005, and "The New York Times and the Jews (2)," July 19, 2006, both, http://www.americanthinker.com.

24. Mearsheimer and Walt, "The Israel Lobby," p. 44.

25. Ibid., pp. 30–31.

26. Ibid., pp. 35.

27. Ibid., p. 32.

28. Eli Lake, "David Duke Claims To Be Vindicated by a Harvard Dean," *New York Sun,* March 20, 2006, p. 1, http://daily.nysun.com/Repository/getFiles.asp?Style=OliveXLib:ArticleToMail&Type=text/html&Path=NYS/2006/03/20&ID=Ar00100.

29. John J. Mearsheimer and Stephen M. Walt, "Setting the Record Straight: A Response to Critics of 'The Israel Lobby,'" *America and the Future,* Spring 2007, Goals for America Foundation, p. 3.

30. Ibid., p. 15.

31. Ibid., p. 23.

32. Ibid., p. 5.

33. David Gergen, "An Unfair Attack," *U.S. News & World Report,* March 26, 2006, http://www.usnews.com/usnews/opinion/articles/060403/3edit.htm.

34. Mearsheimer and Walt, "Setting the Record Straight," pp. 6–7.

35. Ibid., p. 3.

CHAPTER 3

1. John J. Mearsheimer and Stephen Walt, "The Israel Lobby and U.S. Foreign Policy," working paper no. RWP06–011, March 13, 2006, p. 1, *Faculty Research Working Paper Series,* John F. Kennedy School of Government Web site, http://ksgnotes1.harvard.edu/Research/wpaper.nsf/rwp/RWP06–011. p. 11.

2. Walter Laqueur, *The Changing Face of Antisemitism: From Ancient Times to the Present Day* (New York: Oxford University Press, 2006), p. 8.

3. Martin Kramer, "The American Interest: A Realist Case for the U.S.-Israel Alliance," *Wall Street Journal,* Nov. 21, 2006, http://www.opinionhournal.com/forms/printThis.html?id=110009278.

4. George Lardner Jr. and Michael Dobbs, "New Tapes Reveal Depth of Nixon's Anti-Semitism," *Washington Post,* Oct. 6, 1999, p. A31, http://www.washingtonpost.com/wpsrv/politics/daily/oct99/nixon6.htm.

5. Mearsheimer and Walt, "The Israel Lobby," p. 16.

6. Jodie T. Allen and Alec Tyson, "The U.S. Public's Pro-Israel History: In Mid-East Conflicts, Americans Consistently Side with Israel," July 19, 2006, Pew Research Center Publications, http://pewresearch.org/pubs/39/the-us-publics-pro-israel-history.

7. Ibid.

8. Leslie Wayne, "Foreign Sales by U.S. Arms Makers Doubled in a Year," *New York Times,* Nov. 11, 2006, http://select.nytimes. com/search/restricted/article?res=F3061EF6345B0C728DDDA 80994DE404482.
9. Mearsheimer and Walt, "The Israel Lobby," pp. 22–23.
10. "Palestine Solidarity Movement: Backgrounder," Anti-Defamation League Web site, http://www.adl.org/israel/psm.asp. Also see the Palestinian Solidarity Movement Web site, http:// palestinesolidaritymovement.org/index.htm.
11. Tony Judt, "The Country that Wouldn't Grow Up," *Ha'aretz,* May 5, 2006, http://www.haaretz.com/hasen/objects/pages/ PrintArticleEn.jhtml?itemNo=711997.
12. Donald Neff, "Israel Requests $10 Billion in U.S. Loan Guarantees for Soviet Immigrants," *Washington Report on Middle East Affairs,* April/May 1995, http://www.wrmea.com/backissues/ 0495/9504079.htm.
13. Mearsheimer and Walt, "The Israel Lobby, p. 38.
14. Ibid., pp. 37–38.

CHAPTER 4

1. Tony Judt, *Postwar: A History of Europe Since 1945* (New York: Penguin Press, 2005).
2. Tony Judt, "Israel: The Alternative," *New York Review of Books,* Oct. 23, 2003, http://www.nybooks.com/articles./16671.
3. Demographic information drawn from *World Factbook 2007* (Washington, D.C.: The Central Intelligence Agency, 2007). Data for Israel at https://www.cia.gov/cia/publications/factbook/geos/is.html; data for the West Bank at https://www.cia. gov/cia/publications/factbook/geos/we.html.
4. Judt, "Israel: The Alternative."
5. Ibid.
6. Leon Wieseltier, "The Shahid," *New Republic,* Oct. 23, 2006.
7. Robert Frost, in a letter to the *Amherst Student,* 1935. Quoted in "Frost as a Critical Theorist," in Elaine Barry, *Robert Frost on Writing* (New Brunswick, N.J.: Rutgers University Press, 1973), http://www.frostfriends.org/FFL/Frost%20on%20writing%20- %20Barry/barryessay2.html.

8. Tony Judt, "A Lobby, Not a Conspiracy," *New York Times*, April 19, 2006, http://www.informationclearinghouse.info/article127 93.htm.

9. Ibid.

10. Tony Judt, "The Country that Wouldn't Grow Up," *Ha'aretz*, May 5, 2006, http://www.haaretz.com/hasen/objects/pages/ PrintArticleEn.jhtml?itemNo=711997.

11. http://www.network2020.org.site2.php?site=about&child-site=mission.

12. Quoted in Doug Ireland, "Tony Judt Gets Mugged by the A.D.L.," Scholars for Peace in the Middle East Web site, http://www.spme.net/cgi-bin/articles.cgi?ID=1209.

13. "In N.Y., Sparks Fly over Israel Criticism," *Washington Post*, Oct. 8, 2006.

14. "A Statement in Support of Open and Free Discussion about U.S. and Israeli Foreign Policy and Against Suppression of Speech," *Archipelago*, http://www.archipelago.org/vol10–12/ freespeech.htm.

15. Mark Lilla and Richard Sennett, "The Case of Tony Judt: An Open Letter to the ADL," *New York Review of Books*, Nov.16, 2006, http://www.nybooks.com/articles/19550.

16. Ibid.

17. Ibid.

18. Alan Wolfe, "Free Speech, Israel, and Jewish Illiberalism," *Chronicle of Higher Education*, Nov.17, 2006, p. B6.

19. Ibid.

20. Graham Bowley, "Lunch with the FT: Tony Judt," *Financial Times*, March 16, 2007, http://www.ft.com/cms/s/3824ee52-d316–11db–829f–000b5df10621.html.

CHAPTER 5

1. Benjamin Pogrund, "Apartheid? Israel Is a Democracy in Which Arabs Vote," *Focus* 40, Fourth quarter 2005, http://www.hsf.org.za/%23ArticleDatabase/article_view.asp?id=412.

2. Joseph Lelyveld, "Jimmy Carter and Apartheid," *New York Review of Books*, March 29, 2007, pp. 14, 16.

3. Jimmy Carter, *Palestine: Peace Not Apartheid* (New York: Simon & Schuster, 2007), pp.189–90.

4. Lelyveld, "Jimmy Carter and Apartheid," p.14.
5. Carter, *Palestine: Peace Not Apartheid,* pp. 208, 216.
6. Ibid., p.147.
7. Ibid., pp.106–07.
8. Kenneth W. Stein, "My Problem with Jimmy Carter's Book," *Middle East Quarterly,* Spring 2007, http://www.meforum.org/pf.php?id=1633.
9. Carter, *Palestine: Peace Not Apartheid,* pp. 130–131.
10. Stein, "My Problem with Jimmy Carter's Book,"
11. Carter, *Palestine: Peace Not Apartheid,* p. 184.
12. Ibid.
13. "Carter Palestine book spurs resignations: 14 advisory members protest former president's criticism of Israeli policy," Associated Press, Jan.11, 2007, http://www.msnbc.com/id/16579676/.
14. Dennis Ross, "Don't Play with Maps," *New York Times,* Jan. 9, 2007, p. A17.
15. Carter, *Palestine: Peace Not Apartheid,* pp. 152, 154.
16. Bill Clinton, *My Life* (New York: Alfred A. Knopf, 2004), pp. 914–15.
17. Ibid., pp. 943–45
18. Ibid.
19. Ibid.
20. Ibid., p. 924.
21. Carter, *Palestine: Peace Not Apartheid,* ch. 17.
22. Stein, "My Problem with Jimmy Carter's Book."
23. Ibid.
24. Carter, *Palestine: Peace Not Apartheid,* p. 209.
25. Ross, "Don't Play with Maps."
26. Excerpt from Jimmy Carter, "A Letter to Jewish Citizens of America," Dec. 15, 2006, Carter Center Web site, http://www.cartercenter.org/news/pr/carter_letter_121506.html.
27. Glen S. Levy and Abraham H. Foxman, "An Open Letter to Jimmy Carter," Dec. 20, 2006. Available at http://www.adl.org/PresRele/IslME_62/4947_62.htm.
28. Carter, *Palestine: Peace Not Apartheid,* page 26.
29. Jeffrey Goldberg, "What Would Jimmy Do? A former president puts the onus for resolving the Mideast conflict on the Israelis," *Washington Post,* Dec. 10, 2006, p. BW03.
30. Carter, *Palestine: Peace Not Apartheid,* p. 28.

CHAPTER 6

1. Scott Ritter, *Target Iran: The Truth about the White House's Plans for Regime Change* (New York: Nation Books, 2006), pp. 208, 210.
2. Ritter, *Target Iran*, p. 211.
3. David Brooks, "A War of Narratives," *New York Times*, April 8, 2007, http://select.nytimes.com/2007/04/08/opinion/08brooksd.html?n=Top%2fOpinion%2fEditorials%20and%20Op%2dEd%2fOp%2dEd%2fColumnists%2fDavid%20Brooks.
4. Quoted in Kevin Montgomery, "Anti-Semitism Will Not Come to Brandeis," *Brandeis Hoot*, March 9, 2007, http://www.the-hoot.net/?module=displaystory&story_id=1876&edition_id=56&format=html. Copyright © 2007 by The New York Times Co. Reprinted with permission.
5. Jimmy Carter, *Palestine: Peace Not Apartheid* (New York: Simon & Schuster, 2007), p. 209.
6. Tony Judt, "A Lobby, Not a Conspiracy," *New York Times*, April 19, 2006, http://www.informationclearinghouse.info/article12793.htm.

INDEX